The 90-Minute MBA®

For Those Too Busy Doing Things Right
To Do The Right Things

By

Arnold S. Grundvig, Jr.

A-Systems Corporation
Salt Lake City, Utah

ISBN 978-0-9785968-1-1 (Paperback)

Library of Congress Control Number: 2006904336

Published by:

A-Systems Corporation
4141 Highland Drive, Suite 210
Salt Lake City, UT 84124-2656
(800) 365-6790

www.The90MinuteMBA.com

Printed in the United States of America

This book is dedicated to a great lady, my wife, Barbara.

Table of Contents

Introduction

I've had the great fortune of meeting with thousands of entrepreneurs. Most of them went into business with the honorable goal of *doing things right*. Sadly, many of these good people failed in business because they *didn t do the right things*. Addressing that unfortunate reality is how the entrepreneurial seminar, *The 90-Minute MBA*®, came to be. Its goal is to draw attention to key issues that are often missed or *ignored* by the overworked owners and managers of small businesses. In a word, the seminar shares powerful **insights!**

The first time the seminar was presented was in the spring of 2000, hosted by and at the request of the United States Small Business Administration (the SBA). Over 150 people showed up that spring morning—to a room that held only 24. No one at the SBA expected such a large turnout. Since then, *The 90-Minute MBA* has been presented coast-to-coast and border-to-border to great crowds of entrepreneurs. Many of them come to the seminar believing they are doing things right, but not sure they are doing the right things. The seminar focuses them, answers their questions, and shows them what they need to do to *succeed*. At virtually every presentation, "graduates" have requested a copy of *the book* in order to study and absorb the powerful strategies shared in the seminar. That is why this book was published.

In business, just as in sports, success requires the right combination of offensive and defensive strategies, *or* a lot of dumb luck. Few people wish to risk their fortunes to luck of any kind. Fortunately for us, many of the risks of running a small business are as predictable as winter following autumn. Addressing those risks is as essential as preparing for winter, but using only defensive strategies is never sufficient to create success. Entrepreneurs who implement the right offensive strategies in combination with effective defensive strategies are the few who *do the right things*.

It is a sad reality that most of us seem to learn best from experience, often very costly experience. There is no way to count how many times I've heard someone say, "Next time, I'll know better." That's the *hard* way to learn. A degree from "The School of Hard Knocks" is nothing to brag about. A far smarter way is to learn from the successes *and failures* of others. It can save us many sleepless nights, something a friend once called his "nights of terror."

History records that after Christopher Columbus returned to Spain from the New World, he wasn't granted a lot of respect for what he had accomplished. According to one legend, he was the guest of honor at a feast when a cynic mocked him saying, "You didn't do anything that anyone here couldn't have done. All we would have to do is sail west until we bumped into the same land you did."

Columbus listened patiently, then stood and asked each person at the table to take their boiled egg and stand it on its end. Everyone quickly accepted his challenge, but no one could do it. Columbus said, "Now, watch me." Then, he took his boiled egg and thumped it on the table, leaving it standing solidly on one end. He turned to his heckler and said, "Now that I've shown how it's done, *anyone* can do it."

A lot of people have already shown us the right things to do in business. Others have shown us the *wrong* things. We only need to know which are which. In truth, most of what is taught at universities was learned by someone else, somewhere else. Universities concentrate, package, and present, showing us how someone else did it. *The 90-Minute MBA* concentrates, packages, and presents practical insights from the real-world successes and failures of thousands of entrepreneurs. This book is not a collection of case studies, but specific things to do and not do, if you wish to succeed.

Embezzlement

When I present this information in person, I ask those who are business owners or managers to raise their hands. Then, I quickly count how many hands are raised and I ask them to raise their hands again if they "are being embezzled *today*, *right now,* at this very moment?"

In larger groups, there is always at least one hand raised. When the rest of the group notices, there is often a quiet rumbling of sympathetic comments. Before the noise dies down, I offer a surprising statistic. "Research done by the American Institute of Banking suggests that on any given day, one business in four is being embezzled!" After doing a quick calculation, I tell my audience, "That means in this group there are probably x number of you who are being embezzled." Then, pointing to the one (or more) who raised their hands, I add, "*They* are the only ones who know!"

It is a shock to most business owners to learn how many businesses are embezzled. Experts with experience in this area think the rate may be even higher than one in four. Because many are never *detected*, there is just no way to know exactly what the real number is.

One afternoon I was listening to a radio talk show when the guest, a bankruptcy attorney, observed that in his experience, one business in three that goes bankrupt got there because of an embezzler. Unfortunately, I have found no formal research along that line, but it sounds reasonable.

In business, we have to face the reality that literally everyone with employees is at risk. We probably cannot totally eliminate embezzlement, but we can certainly reduce it significantly.

Bear in mind that if you are confident you have nothing to worry about, you may be one of those most likely to be ripped-off. Overconfidence leads to the kind of sloppiness that makes it easy for someone to get away with our money. Those who *are* concerned about embezzlement are more likely to take the kind of precautions that reduce the risk. This is *reality.*

Ask yourself, "*Am I safe? Is there any chance someone could be stealing from my business?*" If you have not examined this possibility, take the time to do it now and don't kid yourself. It is too costly to ignore what might be happening. Far too many entrepreneurs do not discover embezzlement until losses threaten the very survival of their business. By then, it may be too late.

Stories about who got away with how much and what it did to the business are commonplace. Most of the companies that suffered from embezzlement left themselves so obviously vulnerable, it was only a matter of time until the right (or wrong) person came along. All they had to do was take advantage of an easy opportunity. In most cases, embezzlement occurs when desperation meets opportunity.

For a minute, let's imagine ourselves as employees. In real life, we are all faced with times when we just don't have all the money we need. I'm not talking about the "need" for a luxury car or an extended vacation in Europe. I'm talking about just getting by, living from paycheck to paycheck. If a list of bills sneaked up on us all at the same time, we wouldn't have enough money. What if our 12 year-old needed new glasses, the water heater rusted out, the car needed a new transmission, and we needed to fly to St. Louis for Aunt Mary's funeral? There are times when all of us need more money than we can get our hands on.

So, there we are. We're desperate, but we have an untapped resource available to us. We could slip a couple of thousand dollars out of our employer's checking account and no one would notice. After all, we write the checks, we do the bookkeeping, and we even do the bank reconciliation. Besides, we're sure we can pay it back before anyone notices. What's wrong with a quick loan? We convince ourselves that it won't hurt anyone and it will certainly help us out of a jam.

We justify it and go ahead because the sad truth is we have no other option. Time passes quickly and before we can pay anything back, something else comes along and we need to "borrow" more. This story is repeated thousands of times, day after day, in small businesses across the country. The circumstances are different, but the consequences are always the same.

Once an embezzler gets started, it's easy to continue. It's a rare occasion when any money is actually returned. Before long, $100,000 or more is missing and the business is in deep trouble. The embezzler has no way of paying it back. The money is spent. It's gone! It went to a hospital for corrective surgery, or into new tires, or fixing a leaky roof. If we pursue it with every bit of our energy, the only possible outcome is that someone *may* go to jail. But, sending someone to jail *won't* save our business. It won't generate a single penny in payback. However, making the effort to "get even" with an embezzler *will* focus our attention away from the business at the time when it needs us the most. Stop and think. It might make us feel better to get even with the thief, but will it help our business? Will concentrating on it do anything more than canker our soul? We need to do what we can to recover our money and then move on as quickly and as decisively as possible. It will be necessary to put the "hurt" behind us, to unravel that knot in our stomach, the one that came from being betrayed by someone we trusted. We cannot afford to let an embezzler cause us to lose our focus. If we do, we actually multiply the risk of failure.

Our hypothetical embezzler did not start out with the intention of making our business fail. Typical embezzlers were just desperate and settled on what they saw as an easy solution, often the *only* one they had. In most cases, an embezzler was totally trustworthy before that first dishonest act. After that, they changed. They became hard to work with. They seemed cranky. They weren't involved in things the way they used to be, even though they worked lots of late hours (to cover their trail.) They didn't tell jokes like they once did. They became different people. Embezzlement destroyed them and our business.

Of course, there are people with no scruples. When they embezzle, they might even become more outgoing, smoothly leading any conversation away from the discussion of cash shortages to something else, anything else. In the meantime, they might buy a new car and move to an apartment they could never afford if they weren't stealing from us. Maybe I'm an optimist, but I believe most people *are* trustworthy. That is, until they have no other choice and the opportunity is just too easy to resist. Of course, if I'm wrong, that makes the situation even worse. We *must* eliminate as many opportunities to embezzle as we can.

So, how do they get money out of our business? They get creative and then they cleverly cover their tracks. That's the general strategy. Now, let's get specific and see what we can do. If we know *how* they embezzle, we should be better prepared to deal with it. Here are some of the most common methods.

In an oft-repeated scenario, the accounts payable clerk creates a phony invoice from a real or nonexistent vendor and then pays the bill. The check is immediately pocketed by the clerk or it is mailed to an address from which it eventually ends up in the clerk's personal bank account.

Sometimes when embezzlers set up phony vendors, they boldly use their own home address.

We rarely take the time to verify an invoice *after* it is paid, so the trail quickly grows cold and it is soon forgotten. If the accounts payable clerk is smart, the trail is totally eliminated. When the check comes back from the bank, it and the phony invoice are both destroyed. If the bank statement contains no more detail about the check than its number and dollar amount (like banks prefer in this day of electronic transactions), there is nothing to see. If the statement includes an "image" of the check, that page may be "misplaced." Now, the trail is worse than cold, it's gone. Unless you know exactly what you are looking for and where it should be, the embezzlement will *never* be discovered, not even by accident.

In a twist on this scenario, the accounts payable clerk writes a check for "Cash" for say $1,000, and puts the money in his own pocket. A phony invoice from a legitimate vendor is then "posted" (entered into the accounting software) as "Paid by hand check" for $1,000. When the bank statement comes back, the same slight of hand described earlier is repeated and the trail is destroyed. If the hand check is ever looked for, it is just "missing."

In another variation of this strategy, the accounts payable clerk writes a check to himself for $10,000. Then, he uses the accounting system to cover his trail by changing the amount already paid to a legitimate vendor on an earlier check to include his embezzled $10,000. To accomplish this, he has to alter the source document in the accounting software. Of course, the actual $10,000 check *never* makes it back to the file. Once again, there is no trail to follow.

The solution here is to have accounting software that does not allow *anyone* to alter source transactions or documents. Once completed (or posted), transactions should be permanently protected by what professional accountants call an "audit trail." If changes must be made, they should be handled by creating "correcting" entries, not by altering the record of the original transaction. Unfortunately, some kinds of "accounting" software allow individuals to *turn off* the audit trail, so they can alter transactions whenever they please. What a wonderful tool for embezzlers! Can we resist asking the obvious? Who else but the bookkeeper will likely have control of the accounting software *and* who else but the bookkeeper will use the accounting software to cover their tracks? Get rid of that software immediately! Get *real* accounting software, something with a bulletproof audit trail.

Building contractors routinely use something that discourages embezzlement, an accounting process called job costing. It tracks every payment and matches it to an actual *budgeted* expense. Contractors use it to *control* costs. Many of them believe they have a lower rate of embezzlement because of it, but contractors still have problems with embezzlement. There are other things that need to be done. They are simple and we'll cover them one by one.

Here's an embezzlement tactic that hits larger companies. The payroll clerk or a supervisor adds a nonexistent employee to the payroll. These are referred to as "phantom" or "ghost" employees. Many companies have them. When they have one, they usually have several or a series of them. It's too easy to get away with. On rare occasions, the payroll clerk and a supervisor participate in this scheme jointly. This can go on for years before anyone suspects anything. In the meantime, the clerk and the supervisor pocket tax-free money every payday. This is the kind of activity the IRS sends people to jail for. Few embezzlers bother to list "Embezzlement" as "Other Income" on their tax return. Requiring two signatures on each check will discourage much of this, especially if both signers are required to *know* all employees. Warning note: Requiring two signatures does not mean the bank will assume the liability of verifying that two signatures actually *are* on checks. This is an "internal" control only. The company might do well to keep a "log" of checks, initialed by the individuals who signed them. *All* missing or skipped numbers should be accounted for. Voided checks should be marked as "Void" and saved, not destroyed, to be certain they have been voided and not used for embezzlement.

Here's another problem. When there are multiple companies under the same roof, or owned by the same parent company, things can get complicated easily. Intercompany transactions can occur so often and with so little documentation, that only the accounting clerk may know what actually happened (and the clerk may not be that certain most of the time).

In one company, the accountant doing intercompany transactions was also responsible for reconciling them. The balances between the companies were always "in the process" of being reconciled. The accountant used this confusion to cover up cash withdrawals he made to himself. One day, he did not show up for work. The next day he was not there either. A call to his home revealed that he was missing. His wife and family had no idea where he was. Soon, it became apparent that he was not the only thing missing. Over $1 million was gone from the business. The accountant and the money were eventually discovered to be "vacationing" in Brazil. Before this happened, the man was known to be impeccably honest, an icon of virtue, from a family of the highest reputation. No one ever thought he would steal money from his employer. By the way, that business no longer exists. The counter to this is to have all intercompany transactions documented and verified by individuals from the respective companies.

"Petty Cash" disbursements are very easy to falsify. They are often documented, approved, and disbursed by the same person. The amounts are not large individually, but over time, they can amount to a nice pile of money. The label of "petty cash" is misleading. There's nothing *petty* about cash. A little petty cash might be used to pay someone's monthly utilities, buy gasoline, or get new tires for the car. Dipping into petty cash is a convenient way for an embezzler to handle smaller personal financial difficulties.

The clerk at one company foolishly used petty cash to expand her wardrobe and acquire a few toiletries, purchasing whatever she wanted during a visit to Sam's Club. Fortunately, someone else reviewed her purchase and her first attempt at embezzlement was discovered immediately. An easy strategy is to require all petty cash payments to be approved in advance or reviewed after the fact by someone other than the person doing the disbursement.

Another old tactic has the embezzler taking "Less Cash" on a bank deposit, but the teller does not check to see if the depositor is *authorized* to make withdrawals. (This is more likely to happen in smaller businesses, where "personal" type checks and deposit slips are often used.) After years of doing business with customers, bank tellers often know their customers by their first name, so they never take the time to verify their authority to do a withdrawal. This scenario actually occurred when I was a banker. The woman making the bank deposits had been the office manager for a doctor almost as long as he had been in practice. She got away with small "less cash" deposits for decades. Only by accident did the doctor discover what she was doing. He confronted the bank with the withdrawals she had made and the bank was embarrassed to realize that she was not an "authorized signer" on the account. The bank had been doing it for so long that literally every teller in the branch was guilty of this slipup. The bank immediately reimbursed the doctor for everything he claimed to have lost, something in excess of $30,000. I was not part of the confrontation, but I suspect that he also could have received a nice chunk of interest on his money if he had insisted on it.

So, how is embezzlement discouraged? Notice that I didn't ask, "How is it prevented?" A determined thief will find a way to steal, even if it is slipping office supplies home in a briefcase or hauling lumber from a construction site. The best controls are in simple precautions that keep honest employees honest and make it more difficult for the rest.

The most effective strategy to reduce our company's exposure to embezzlement is to *separate* the tasks that embezzlers use to *take* money from the tasks used to *cover* their tracks. Individual cash handling processes should be performed by as many different individuals as possible. The more the steps are broken up, the lower the risk of loss.

So, how can we protect ourselves when the accounting, receivables, payroll, and payables "departments" are only one person? The first thing to do is have the bank statement mailed to our home address. When it comes, it should be *opened* and *every* check reviewed. Check the payee, see if the amounts are right, and verify that two people have signed each check. Deposits should be reviewed for anything suspicious. We need to know.

Second, we must get involved at key steps, signing two-signature checks, keeping a log of *all* checks, approving payments, and/or doing the bank reconciliation. One businessman has his wife, an experienced accountant, do the monthly bank reconciliation. That is his only control. He feels he is adequately covered. Perhaps. How does she know the checks were paid against legitimate invoices?

Another executive reviews a list of reports each day to monitor cash income and expenses, verifying any suspicious items. Unfortunately, reports can be faked to show different names and numbers than what really happened. Checks may be written to one person and "posted" into the accounting system to another person or company. This is where a log of checks signed by approved signers might prove useful. It depends on how your office runs.

The owner of one small business does the cash accounting, personally opening her mail and making the bank deposit, while having a clerical staff support her by entering the transactions into the accounting software. This can be effective for the receivables side, if we have the time. Another entrepreneur has the secretary open all the mail, then prepare and make the bank deposit. Someone else does the actual accounting.

After one manager caught an employee creating duplicate accounts payable checks, sending one to the vendor while keeping the second check for herself, he developed an internal control that he is satisfied with. He keeps a spreadsheet, a log of all checks and deposits that he has personally verified or signed, a step beyond the basic check log described earlier. He follows that by doing a bank reconciliation each morning. Almost every bank allows "online banking," so this effort takes only a few minutes. It works for him and he sleeps well at night.

Each solution is as unique as the situation. The strategy is to reduce the opportunities to steal *and* eliminate the ways of covering up the theft. In general, each of the following steps should be performed by as many different people as possible or the sequential steps separated and shared as much as possible.

- Entering accounts receivable invoices into the accounting software
- Preparing and mailing invoices
- Opening the mail

- Preparing and making the bank deposit
- Entering receipts into the accounting software
- Doing the bank reconciliation for the operating account
- Creating purchase orders
- Approving invoices for payment
- Coding and entering accounts payable invoices into the accounting software
- Signing accounts payable checks (or requiring two signatures)
- Adding new employees into the accounting software
- Approving timesheets for payment
- Entering timesheets into the accounting software
- Signing payroll checks (or requiring two signatures)
- Ordering blank check stock
- Doing the bank reconciliation for the payroll account
- Printing W-2s and 1099s
- Doing petty cash disbursement, documentation, and account coding

This list focuses on distinct steps within the accounting process, but there is more that can be done. We covered the need to have an audit trail in our accounting software. In addition, we need accounting software that compares *actual* expenditures to *budgeted* amounts and calculates variances between the two, much like the job costing process used by contractors. This requires us to have a budget. For some people, this looks like a challenge, but it is quite simple. It takes time, but it is time well spent. The side effect is something we'll discuss in another section, *Cost Control*. For now, it is enough to say that when actual costs exceed the budgeted amount, we need to know why.

Implementing these suggestions will discourage most honest employees, but what about the others? If it takes two people to successfully embezzle money, it requires two people to confess their dishonesty to each other. Often, the need to recruit an accomplice is a strong deterrent because of social pressure. Still, it sometimes happens that two people will conspire to rip off the company. These are not honest people who were presented with an easy opportunity which they took advantage of in a moment of desperation. Duplicity requires the mindset of a thief, not a desperate employee.

Thieves are much more difficult to deter. Usually they are experienced and clever. If we were to call their references, their prior employer would probably refuse to talk to us or just give vague answers to our questions. They are afraid to tell the truth because the "rights" of the guilty have become more important than the rights of the victims in the upside-down, politically correct silliness of our times. We do not know whom we can trust.

Years ago when I was working for Dun & Bradstreet, I was writing a credit report on a furniture retailer in northern Utah. This man's credit rating was destroyed when his brother, who handled the financial side of the business, left town with all the money he could get his hands on. When the owner of the business discovered what had happened, his accountant and his attorney counseled him that bankruptcy was his only logical course of action. He refused. He felt that his creditors had trusted him. *He* was the one that had trusted his brother, so it wasn't their problem; it was his. He resolved to pay them back ($140,000, if my memory is accurate). It took him several years to do it, but he did. When he recovered, it was my privilege to reassign his good credit rating. He deserved it. He earned it. What was his response when I told him his good credit rating was being restored? Tears filled his eyes and he swallowed to keep his voice from breaking. In addition to being a financial trial, embezzlement is an emotional experience because we were betrayed by someone we trusted.

There's another point to this story. This man was ripped-off by his own brother! When we ask, "Who's at risk?" The answer is that *everyone* is at risk.

There are several versions of this next story, so we wonder if it is more "urban legend" than reality. In one version, the owner of a bar believed the bartenders were stealing from him, so he hired a security firm. They sent people called "secret shoppers" to watch the bartenders. They confirmed that all of the sales were being rung up. All of the money always went into one of the registers. Correct change was always given. Tips were kept in beer mugs behind the bar. No money was put into the bartender's pockets. They did not have a clue how it was being done. Of course, they were drinking alcohol while this was going on, so the owner of the bar was less than confident in their assurances. He installed security cameras and paid a security firm to watch the monitors (without drinking). They reported that the accountant personally picked up each of the five cash registers one at a time to count the money each day and they verified what the "secret shoppers" had reported. They still didn't have a clue.

In the end, someone accidentally discovered that the bartenders had purchased their own cash register. There were *six* registers along the counter. Five belonged to the business and one belonged to the bartenders. Bold and creative!

To summarize, everyone with employees is at risk all the time. We can implement simple ideas to reduce our risk. If we do not follow through, we are still at risk, we will pay the consequences, and like it or not, it is *our fault* when we are embezzled.

This issue demands attention, not denial. Ignoring the risk of embezzlement only increases the likelihood that it will damage or destroy our business. Ignoring the possibility of embezzlement is like that old saying, "putting your head in the sand." May I ask, where is your butt when you put your head in the sand? This is not a good position to be in! Embezzlement is a land mine located in every business. It must be addressed.

Profit versus Cash

There is a difference between Profit and Cash. Everyone knows (or should know) this, but sometimes we don't remember why or we get the two terms confused. An example might sound like this:

"My accountant says I made money, but I can t pay the bills. What am I doing wrong?"

Here is the answer: Cash pays bills, not profit. Everyone knows what cash is. It's money. "Profit" is the confusing word. Profit is an accounting term. For tax purposes, we often use "accrual" accounting. Accrual accounting means that we account for income *before* we receive payment and we account for expenses *before* we pay them. We do this so we can comply with the accounting "ideal" of matching income and expenses, recognizing them in the fiscal period (usually the month) in which they were actually earned or incurred. Accrual accounting is the best tool we have to accurately calculate profitability. As important as profitability is, it has very little to do with cash flow. This is the source of the confusion.

One way to eliminate the difference would be to use "cash basis" accounting, where we would not recognize income until we are paid. Likewise, we would not recognize expenses until we pay them. This is a terrible way to calculate profitability or to know "how we did last month." If you want to *accurately* track profitability, accrual accounting is the right tool. We need to remember that information from accrual accounting will *never* match actual cash flow.

Consider this accrual accounting scenario to demonstrate the concept. The first thing this morning, the Sales Manager turned in an order for $50,000. Later in the day, the order was efficiently shipped from inventory. The accountant reports that we "booked" revenue of $50,000. We recognized a cost of goods sold of $30,000, so we showed a profit of $20,000. That's what happened in the accounting world. In the physical world, where we live and breathe, we have $30,000 less in inventory, so we need to restock, but we still owe $30,000 on the inventory we just shipped. We don't have any more cash than we did yesterday, but we *might* get paid $50,000 in the next month or so from this sale. On payday, the Sales Manager will need to be paid a commission and we will need to order more inventory immediately. We still have real bills to pay, but the "profit" showing on our "bottom line" will not be "cash" for some time.

Cash flow versus profit is an important concept. It deserves this entire chapter, all to itself, in order to emphasize the point.

So, how do we make ends meet when sales do not generate immediate cash flow? We plan ahead. We need to know if we have enough money to be in business. How much cash will it take? The answers to these questions are answered in two words, "Cash Management."

Cash Management

Cash Management used to be known as budgeting. As individuals, we use budgeting to warn us in advance if we don't have enough money to pay our bills as they come due. If there isn't enough money, not only can we *not* afford to buy that progressive-scan DVD player and the surround-sound system we've been looking at, we may not be able to afford a trip to the grocery store. The same concepts apply to our business.

Of course at home, we all know that we don't need real money if we have a credit card. (This traditional delusion has caused many personal bankruptcies and destroyed many marriages.) In business, the misuse of debt will cause a business to fail just as quickly as it will destroy a marriage. Many people drive their businesses into the ground because they try to finance operating costs with expensive credit, the way foolish people run their lives. That's a harsh statement, but if you are offended perhaps it's time to evaluate your cash management habits.

Here are some hard questions: If we don't manage our cash…

- How can we track how much cash we *have*?
- How can we know how much cash we *expect* to receive and when?
- How can we know how much cash we *need* to have, day by day?

If we don't manage our cash…

- How do we know where we *are* versus where we *planned* to be?
- How do we know where we *need to be*?

In 1974, I created a cash management budget on a simple spreadsheet. When I say "simple," I'm not exaggerating. In 1974, there were no electronic spreadsheets, just pencil and paper. Even handheld calculators were new.

One day, a lady working in my office complained that her ex-husband saved up his alimony and child support, only to pay her a huge lump sum every six months. She complained that by the time she got the money, she was so far behind that she used every penny to pay off the debt she had accumulated over the prior six months. She wanted to know how to get by without going into debt until the next check came in. She said she was willing to make whatever effort it would take to break this cycle.

I used an ordinary calendar to create a basic cash management system. The concept was simple, add up all of your income, subtract your expenses, and spread whatever is left over the days of the month. In spite of (or perhaps because of) its simplicity, it works.

She gave me a list of all the payments she had to make, how much they were, and what day she paid them. They went on the calendar as "minus" amounts, on the days she actually planned to pay them. She listed how much money she needed for rent, to buy groceries, pay utilities, and so on. She also included the "minimum" payments on her credit accounts. Next, her take-home pay went on the calendar as "plus" amounts on the days she was paid. All numbers were based on the actual *day* cash came in or was paid out.

Using those numbers, we calculated that her "fixed" or scheduled expenses used all but $210 of her monthly take home pay. If she spread that $210 evenly over the month, she had $7 per day left as "spending money." We defined "spending money" as everything that was not listed on the calendar; gas for the car, clothes, fast food, etc. Remember this was 1974, before the Jimmy Carter years of hyperinflation when the prime rate skyrocketed to 21%. A daily allowance of $7 went a lot further than it does now. It was enough to fill a gas tank. We wrote"-$7" on each day of the calendar for her "daily" spending money. That accounted for every penny of income and outgo. It was a "break-even" cash flow with no surplus or deficit.

The final step was to write how much money she had in her checking account at the top of the starting day, Day 1 on the calendar, and then calculate "Ending Cash" balances for each day. She subtracted $7 from her starting cash and wrote in the amount at the bottom of the day. That was her Ending Cash for Day 1. For the next day, she added what her take-home pay was, subtracted her daily $7, and subtracted the amount she expected to pay for rent. She wrote the Ending Cash number at the bottom of Day 2. That number, Ending Cash, was the one she needed to watch. If she were "on" budget, she would have that much or more left in her checking account. She repeated this calculation for every day on the calendar. It was that simple.

She was surprised to see that she had a negative $12 the day before her second payday of the month. This concerned her. She pointed to this as the reason she was always going into debt. I assured her there was an alternative. She knew in advance when she was going to run out of money and how much she needed. She had time to adjust. In reality, she would not be spending *exactly* $7 a day, every day, day after day. What the cash budget told her was that she needed to cut her expenditures by a mere $12 sometime between now and the day she was going to run short of money. She thought for only a moment and concluded that, "If I have $7 a day to spend on things like gasoline, clothes, and junk food, all I need to do is *not spend* my $7 for two days and I'll have it made." She was right.

She mastered the concept immediately because it was so simple.

What her cash budget showed was how much money she actually had, how much money she needed, and most importantly, whether she needed to make adjustments in her spending habits. She soon reported that the first thing she learned was that she had a habit of spending a lot of money for things she could get along without. (Like she's different from the rest of us?) The second surprise was how *easy* it was to stop spending money for things of little worth. She actually had extra cash every week, not a lot, but a little. Remember, this was only on $7 per day. The third concept was like a light going on above her head. She took this little surplus and starting *paying off* her debts. She paid off the smallest debt first, her account at a clothing store. Next, she paid off the balance at the doctor's office. She was gaining such a feeling of being in control of her life that a bit of a personality change took place. She was much more confident than before. She smiled more—a lot more. She could even be caught singing to herself now and then.

For several weeks, she would come to my office and report her status every few days or so. Then, she stopped talking about it. I worried that she had busted her cash budget and was ashamed to admit it, so I didn't ask. After about five months, she asked me to come out to the parking lot with her and see something. She was driving a new (used) car. Her old Mustang was nearly dead and she had been complaining that she needed a new car. Then, the shocker, she told me she paid cash for the new car when her ex-husband finally made his semi-annual payment. She said she was now totally debt free and she owed it all to me. She said, "I just wanted you to see what your cash budget did for me."

What worked for her, worked well for me too. I used the cash budgeting system for several years, replacing the calendar with a columnar pad. In 1983, I bought my first PC, along with a new electronic spreadsheet called Lotus®. I moved my cash management system from my columnar pad to my new PC. It was fast, flexible, and very powerful.

About this time, the technical-minded owners of a small business recruited me to handle the financial side of their operation. The first thing I did was to adapt my cash management system to handle the business's cash flow. It worked beautifully. I was able to foresee cash shortages literally months in advance. This allowed plenty of lead-time to deal with forecasted problems. Believe me, working with "technical experts" meant that there were plenty of opportunities to deal with cash flow problems. I used the spreadsheet as an effective cash management tool. As we reduced costs and improved collections, the business soon generated a positive cash flow. We even accumulated a small reserve, a "cash cushion." (This should be one of the first goals for all small businesses.)

A few years later, when I returned to school to earn an MBA, one of members of my MBA group was the manager of a small venture capital firm. I gave him a copy of my spreadsheet format and he used it to do cash management for several companies. He liked what he saw and in 1989 he wrote his master's thesis on it. The title of his thesis was "Cash pays bills, not profit!"

So, why did I go into such a detailed explanation to make a single point? Some people overlook the obvious because it seems too simple. We need to do cash management! What follows is a sample spreadsheet that demonstrates how a simple cash flow budget is designed. As a tool, it works equally well at home or at our business.

1	2	3	4	5	6	7	8
		Cash					Ending
Date	Day	Income	Expense	Explanation	Expense	Explanation	Cash
1	**M**	**Holiday**					**12,876.98**
2	**T**	**5,878**	**12,548**	**Payroll**	**4,405**	**Tax Deposit**	**1,801.98**
3	**W**	**2,288**	**4,055**	**A/P**			**34.98**
4	**Th**	**2,214**					**2,248.98**
5	**F**	**6,678**					**8,926.98**
6	**S**						**8,926.98**
7	**S**						**8,926.98**
8	**M**	**6,501**					**15,427.98**
9	**T**	**5,247**	**17,770**	**A/P**			**2,904.98**
10	W	4,500					7,404.98
11	Th	4,500					11,904.98
12	F	4,500	7,500	A/P			8,904.98
13	S						8,904.98
14	S						8,904.98
15	M	4,500					13,404.98
16	T	4,500	12,500	Payroll	4,400	Tax Deposit	1,004.98
17	W	4,500					5,504.98
18	Th	4,500					10,004.98
19	F	4,500	2,500	A/P			12,004.98

- Column 1 is the day of the month.
- Column 2 is the name of the day of the month.
- Column 3 is the cash actually deposited (or budgeted for deposit).
- Column 4 & 6 are amounts spent (or budgeted to be spent) that day.
- Column 5 & 7 are explanations of the amounts in column 4 & 6.
- Column 8 is the cash balance at the end of the day.

  Column 8 is the only calculated number. It takes the dollar amount above it, adds the cash income from column 3 and subtracts the expenses paid in columns 4 and 6.

Notice the underline that crosses the page beneath Tuesday, January 9th. All numbers up to and including

January 9th are *actual* amounts. The numbers after the 9th are *forecasted* amounts. Each day, the actual dollar amounts are entered, overwriting the forecasted numbers. As actual amounts are entered, the spreadsheet will automatically recalculate "Ending Cash" for future days. Ending Cash is the number to monitor. Negative amounts in the Ending Cash column need to be addressed in advance by using cash management strategies, controlling costs, delaying payments, possibly by borrowing, etc.

After working on one turn-around company for several months, the financial situation was becoming stable. Incompetent management had nearly bankrupted the company, but it was back on course, the course I had charted and kept. By then, the company had a positive cash flow, the debt was totally restructured, and there was a small, but growing cash cushion. Revenue and expenses were very predictable and easily budgeted.

The problem was that the same management that created the original problem still had unfettered decision-making authority. They had the same attitude toward cash that had caused the problem in the first place. The president and vice president of the company became very interested in the cash surplus; apparently the first one they had ever seen. Like children at a cookie jar, they decided to grant themselves a *retroactive* salary increase. They came into my office to divvy up the spoil. They offered to share some of the loot with me, but I declined. I was almost in shock. I couldn't believe what was happening. In a matter of seconds they successfully depleted the only cash reserve the business had ever seen. That was not the worst part. Their salary increases were enough to put the cash flow back to a negative number. That's where they had been when I came to the company to bail them out. They assured each other that I would be able to handle it. After all, I did it once, so I could certainly do it again. What they were saying was that being responsible was my duty, not theirs. After months working many 10 to 16-hour days, I had done all I could or *would* do for them. The benefits of my work were totally dissipated in a moment of greed.

My cash flow forecast showed that the negative cash flow would eliminate the remaining operating cash in about 90 days. There would not be enough money to make payroll on July 15th. I presented my conclusion to members of the board of directors, but they refused to confront the officers or deal with this inevitable reality. They didn't "want to cause an ugly scene." Nothing was going to be done to head off what I considered to be the inevitable outcome of their shortsighted actions. I suggested that bankruptcy would be more ugly than any heart-to-heart talk about management responsibility, but my opinion was ignored.

I concluded that if I were to successfully pull the company out of the fire a second time, it would probably result in management enjoying another "feeding frenzy" at the cash trough. Rather than miss another night's sleep over their foolishness, I left them to their inevitable fate. I packed up my computer and took it home. I called the CPA and handed over all the financial information. Then, I had my phone unlisted, and I waited.

As predicted, there was not enough money to make payroll on July 15th. As expected, the cost of ignoring the consequences of their actions was the eventual failure of the business. Creditors, employees, and shareholders all lost on the deal. Months of work to save the business were wasted because the officers and the board of directors refused to address the reality predicted by the cash flow budget.

Using cash flow budgets can save our businesses. It can warn us of probable situations long before they become problems. Knowledge *is* power! Knowing what is going to happen gives us the power to deal with it in advance, before it becomes a crisis.

If the officers and board of directors of that defunct business had heeded the advanced warning given by the cash flow budget, they would never have lost their investment. By now, the officers could have sold out and retired comfortably. That didn't happen, but it could have. And, it should have.

Accounting

Let's talk about our accountants. Some people consider accounting to be a necessary evil. Others consider it to be the key to their success. Done properly, it is clearly the key to our success. Done poorly, it is not only evil; it can destroy our business.

That's another reality that sounds harsh. How could bad accounting destroy a business? The first answer can be found by reviewing the chapter on embezzlement. Other answers are better illustrated by examples.

- A computer peripherals wholesaler, owned by two technical experts, relied on a "friend" to do their accounting. Because of the friend's preoccupation with personal problems, he did a terrible job of keeping the books. Sometimes, he would pay an invoice and then duplicate the payment when the monthly statement was received. He would invoice companies for certain sales, double invoice for some sales, and never invoice other sales at all. He tracked cash balances by calling the bank to see what the bank showed! The business owners did not require this accountant to provide them with current financial information. They were computer "geeks" who did nothing to monitor the "business" side of their business. They focused all of their attention on the technical side of the operation. As a consequence, their business failed. The bank had no alternative but to foreclose on their loan, the one secured by the home of the president of the company. The accountant caused the problem, but management failed to prevent it by requiring timely financial reporting. In the end, management was at fault and management paid the price.

- A small company in Idaho used the least expensive accountant they could find to do their books. Doing their "books" was not just an accounting expression to him. He kept actual journals in hardback books. Once a year, he "closed the books" and started new ones. I visited him in January of 1973 to obtain a financial statement for the company's credit report. The accountant, aged 75 or older, handed me the journals and said that if I wanted a financial statement, I would have to create it from "the books." I had never seen actual "books" and "journals" except in my accounting textbook. What was worse was that the owner of the business only saw financial statements once a year and those were buried in his tax return. The rest of the time he managed his business by the seat of his pants. If knowledge is power, is ignorance impotence?
- One small company with collections problems disclosed that they used columnar pads to track accounts receivable. The company owned good accounting software, but the "bookkeeper" did not use it to track accounts receivable. This should be a red flag to anyone concerned about the tactics of embezzlers. When I audited receivables, I found amounts from some customers were well over a year past due! The rest were in total disarray. I promptly

computerized receivables and collected thousands of dollars within a week, all from accounts that were over six months past due. The "bookkeeper" was soon history, quitting in a fit of temper. Had the bookkeeper been embezzling? There were several indications that this was the case. With the approval of the board of directors, I researched and verified the company's *current* financial status, but did not audit the history or document the probable embezzlement. It would have been a waste of time to track down what was missing and it would have distracted me from the more important task of reviving the struggling company before it failed.

- In the third quarter of the year, the "Office Manager" of one small business reported that the most current financial information on the company was from December of the prior year. This is another red flag for a possible embezzlement situation. When a new owner took control of the company, the office manager quit over what she described as undue "interference" with the way she did her job—another red flag for embezzlement. When an internal audit was performed, accounting errors totaling $57,000 were uncovered. The audit also turned up numerous personal purchases made with company funds. If prior owners had required current financial statements and had been managing cash flow properly, the situation would have been different.
- A young man called the technical support line of our software company to ask questions about

how to do a payroll on our accounting software. He was doing the accounting for his father's construction company. It turned out that the kid was only 14 years old! He explained that his dad said he was "good with computers and stuff." Here's a secret: Being good at video games does not mean that accounting processes are a "natural." In fact, expertise at video games may not imply the ability to do anything of consequence in the real world. This boy had corrupted the company's accounting data when he "played around" trying to figure out how to do the payroll. Then, when he tried to restore good data from a backup, he erased the backup data too! Running a business means having a competent accountant or bookkeeper. It is not child's play.

- A contractor called our office to complain that he had just finished a job that lost money. The owner said that the job was budgeted to make $100,000, but when everything was paid and all the dust settled, there was a $120,000 loss. That was a $220,000 variance. The contractor was worried, not about the $120,000 loss, but the overall situation. He had no clue where things went wrong. He had no idea if he would do it again on the next job. We introduced him to job cost accounting (using our software, of course). It saved his business and his business is now very profitable. We believe he sleeps better at night too.
- An international operation with a huge accounting staff routinely took at least ninety days to "close the books" month after month.

> The business had numerous operational and financial problems, which were quietly attributed to the accuracy (and lack of timeliness) of their accounting reports. The headquarters of the company were relocated to Utah and a totally new accounting staff took control. Within a few months, the new accounting office reduced monthly closings to ten days, something the original accounting staff insisted was impossible. They accused the new office of sacrificing accuracy for speed. In actual fact, the timely information provided by the new staff was far more accurate than the 'aged" data generated by the original staff. The new staff did things right *the first time*, so they didn't need three months to redo it over and over and over. In addition, because the information was timely, it was far more useful. Before long, the company increased its profits to record levels. Was there a connection? Management thought so.

The 10th of the month is a day every business should look forward to. Every business should "close" its books by the 10th of the following month or as close to it as possible. Financial statements should then be reviewed to answer the important questions:

- Did we make money last month?
- How much have we got in receivables?
- How much is past due?
- What is happening with problem receivables?
- Are our payables past due?
- Are we missing any discounts?
- How do our operating results reconcile with the budget?
- Is inventory adequate for anticipated sales?

- Do we have the cash to meet scheduled debt payments?

Each company should have a list of questions that should be asked and answered on the 10th of the month. We need to keep current with what is happening. We need to know *where we are* and *where we are going.* Again, knowledge *is* power.

There is an old story about an airline pilot coming over the loudspeaker to announce that the gyroscopic compass was not working. He said, "The good news is that we have a powerful tailwind, so we're making excellent time. The bad news is that we're not exactly sure where we're headed." That could be a fair description of a growing business that is not keeping its accounting current.

This is a fact: Accountants are worth their weight in gold, but only if they are more than "bean counters." They have to understand the business and they have to communicate their insights to the owners of the business. Accounting *data* is not accounting *information.*

When I worked for Dun & Bradstreet, I received thousands of financial statements that I put into credit reports. Too often, business owners would hand me their financial statements and ask, "*What do those numbers mean? They don t make any sense to me.*" First, this betrayed a lack of expertise that we will cover later in the chapter called *The Trap.* Second, it points out a communication problem. Some accountants may need to be forced to talk to their clients, not just provide papers filled with numbers. In the chapter *Profit versus Cash,* we quoted a frustrated business owner saying, "*My accountant says I made money, but I can t pay the bills. Am I doing something wrong?*" We need to recognize that having *data* is not enough. It must be converted to *information* before we can use it to run our business.

Legend has it that there was a man riding in a hot air balloon in Europe when a strong wind carried him quickly away and into the clouds. A couple of hours later as he approached the ground, he knew he was lost. He saw someone riding a bicycle and yelled down for help.

"Can you tell me where I am?" he yelled.

The man on the ground stopped and responded, "You are in a yellow balloon."

He yelled again, "Where exactly am I?"

The man on the ground said, in a matter of fact manner, "You are about 15 meters above the ground."

He yelled again, "I mean, precisely where on earth are we? Both of us, now?"

The man on the ground said, "Precisely, you are over a cornfield, on a hillside, three kilometers from town and I'm just beneath you. You are headed west with the wind. In another few minutes you will cross a deep valley with a river running through it."

He yelled down, "Are you an accountant?"

The man on the ground asked, "Yes, I am. How did you know?"

"Everything you tell me is totally accurate, but absolutely worthless."

And so it is with some accountants, the ones we don't need, the ones that provide data and not information. In order to succeed, we need to go one step further than just keeping our books current. We need to be able to compare our actual costs against our budgeted costs. Accounting goes hand in hand with *Cash Management*. This combination produces the kind of knowledge that helps our business succeed.

A-Systems Corporation develops accounting software for small and medium sized businesses. I mention this because we have a unique perspective on the value of accounting. One of our programs uses the powerful accounting process described earlier, called "job costing." It is a sophisticated tool, essential to the success of construction companies. Construction companies that do not use job costing are condemned to remain small or to fail. Realistically, those are the only options. Someone in the construction industry told me, "We have a word for contractors that don't use job costing, 'Bankrupt!'"

Does that sound harsh too? Sure. Reality is like gravity; it can be brutal and unforgiving. In fact, even using job costing is not enough to save people who don't know how to run a construction business. Accounting will make that reality evident, but accounting is just one of the tools necessary to succeed in construction—or any business.

Let me expand on the concept of "job cost accounting" to show how beautifully the process tracks budgets versus actual costs. If this same concept were applied to general business, it could be a powerful management tool. Imagine that we are building a 20-story tower that will take over two years to complete. There are thousands of purchases of material, tens of thousands of individual tasks to be performed, numerous subcontractors who will contribute work and bill us for services, and a myriad of other details to track. Can a construction company wait until the job is over and all these details have been taken care of to find out if it made or lost money? The answer is obviously, "No!" We know what can happen just from the experience of one contractor.

How can a construction company track every phase of a job, each with its own budget in dollars, hours, yards of concrete, feet of wire, etc. as the job progresses? The answer is job costing. On any given day, contractors using job costing know the status of every phase of every job they are doing. This information includes the "cost to complete" every phase and whether that phase is over or under budget. They don't have to wait until the job is over to see if they made money. The beauty of job costing is that it is a simple process. Every phase of the job has its own "mini budget" and actual costs are accumulated against that mini budget. Imagine the difference it could make if other businesses forecasted and monitored their costs in that kind of detail.

Back to that 20-story tower we described. We just finished the 10th floor and our crew reports that it has already installed all of the doors that were delivered to the job site. What do we do? We order more doors. Without job costing we would not know why we ran out of doors and we would get to the end of the job only to discover profits were off by $480,000 for an unknown reason. With job costing we would discover that the plans have openings for 96 doors on each floor, but the specs from the architectural/engineering firm listed only 48 doors. Our estimator used that list of specs and budgeted for 48 doors. Job cost accounting would eventually disclose that 96 doors were actually being installed. The variance would begin to stick out as soon as the 49th door was installed—on the first floor.

When the variance was discovered, the plans might be reviewed and the error by the architectural/engineering firm would be obvious. As the builder, we would call the owner of the building and say, "We have a problem!"

We would then offer to put in the 48 doors specified by the A/E firm and leave the rest of the doorways wide open or we might accept a "Change Order" for 48 more doors per floor. This would increase our income by $480,000. The owner, of course, wants the doors, so he signs the $480,000 "Change Order." He then promptly calls the A/E firm and tells them their "Errors and Omission Insurance" is going to be called upon to pay that additional $480,000. Eventually, an overworked clerk in the back office of an engineering firm says that he counted the doorways on one side of the "U" shaped building, but forgot to multiply the number by two. He is blamed for a simple "counting" error and he loses his job. Using true job cost accounting (and budgeting) saved our construction company a cool $480,000.

Not using true job costing means the company may be using a $300 generic accounting program from the department store. They probably saved somewhere between $3,000 and $8,000 by not purchasing true job cost accounting software. (If they paid more than that, they probably bought over-priced software from a very expensive "consultant.")

When their accountant (worth his weight in gold) finally convinced the owner of the company to purchase the job cost accounting software he truly needed, he probably had to overcome the owner's stiff resistance. The owner probably complained about paying $5,000 for a tool that could save his business, while he sat in his $40,000 pickup with $20,000 worth of specialized tools in the $2,000 toolbox. Accounting software is a tool, an important tool that cannot be ignored by responsible business owners. My dad always told me to "use the right tool for the job." If we're serious about business, we cannot afford to improvise with our accounting tool.

This little side trip into construction accounting was included because construction is the highest risk industry in the economy. Building contractors use budgeting *and* accounting to track and control costs and, in short, to succeed. Contractors provide a perfect illustration of how these processes can be combined to reduce risk. *All* businesses can benefit from good budgeting and accounting.

Payroll

What about payroll? Can (or dare) we do it ourselves? At A-Systems, we often hear this question from prospective clients. Frankly, most people are intimidated by the IRS. They fear they "will be sent to jail for doing something wrong," as one man expressed it. On paydays, some people feverishly struggle with a calculator and books filled with tax schedules, trying to figure out how much to withhold from paychecks. Those who do this have described it as an error prone effort at best. In desperation, others give up and yield control of their payroll to a payroll service.

Is there an alternative? If we can follow instructions, we can do our own payroll. What does it take? The answer is that it takes good payroll software and a checklist of items to pay and when to pay them. It's simply a matter of learning what the IRS, your state, and locality require of you, setting it up in your payroll software, and then paying your taxes on time. FYI: The IRS has different tax deposit requirements, depending on how big your deposits are. See IRS Publication 15 (Circular E) for specifics.

The great thing about software is that it is an ideal tool for doing sophisticated number-crunching tasks like payroll withholding calculations. Even poor accounting programs should look up the correct withholding amount for each employee. There is something to be said for keeping payroll in-house and *controlling* our costs.

What about payroll services? They perform a service and they charge fees, increasing our costs. There is nothing wrong with them, so long as their employees don't make the same mistakes our employees might make. My experience with payroll services hasn't been that good. They are staffed by ordinary people, doing ordinary data entry, just like our companies are. And, here's the final reality, our employees will probably end up doing the data entry into their accounting software anyway. That's how they know what to pay our employees. So, we can still make mistakes, even using a payroll service.

So, this triggers the obvious question: Does the IRS forgive mistakes? We respond bluntly: *Do pigs fly?* There is no room for error when dealing with the IRS!

Several years ago, the congress interrogated victims of IRS bullying tactics as they tried to create a "kinder, gentler" IRS. So what? They could make hundreds of new laws, but it will not matter. The IRS is an organization of people and, like every other organization, it's the people and what they do that counts. The culture at the IRS has been intimidation and threat. It works, so why would they ever change?

When I was a commercial banker, the operations manager received a legal document from the IRS ordering the bank to *seize* a certain company's cash. Someone laughingly referred to this document as a "writ of habeas snatchem," but it's no laughing matter. The IRS order did not ask for a particular amount. It asked how much cash was in the company's accounts and instructed the bank to seize it—*all* of it! The bank immediately followed instructions and took the full amount. That meant that the bank could no longer honor checks that the customer had written, even those dated before the seizure order. The bank completed the necessary paperwork and reported back to the IRS, indicating the amount that had been seized. Of course, the bank manager promptly called our customer to let them know that the IRS had taken their money.

As might be expected, the business owner was livid. His business and the IRS had a running dispute over something that he was firmly convinced was an IRS error. Their discussions were ongoing and the IRS had given no indication they were going to pull a sneak attack. The amount in dispute was a mere $1,100. The amount seized that day was *$67,000.* Of course, the bank was not informed of the amount the IRS needed. The IRS wanted it all, so that's what it got.

I asked the bank manager about the obvious injustice of the situation and was informed that if the bank had not taken it all, the bank would be liable for any shortfall. I was told that if the bank had taken $66,900 and left $100 in the account, and the amount the IRS wanted from our customer turned out to be $1 million, the bank would be required to pay the difference. Banks do not take risks like that! People who play games with the IRS are on their own. It is just foolish to think otherwise. This incident is one reason why it is a good idea to have accounts at more than one bank. We'll discuss more about that later.

It's a good idea to do our taxes as if the tax collector were looking over our shoulder. At one presentation, someone suggested that we should amend that to include that they are looking over our shoulder—while holding a gun to our head. No matter what kind of attitude we might have about the IRS, it is wise to act as if the IRS has the power of life and death over our business and that they are just looking for an excuse to kill it. No matter what the law is or who is enforcing it, the incredible power wielded by the IRS is undeniable. The IRS has closed more than one business. It is up to us to recognize that reality and deal with it rationally. Ignoring it will not make it go away.

It is apparently a temptation for certain businesses that are cash poor to get loans from the IRS. How do they do that? They don't make their tax deposits on time, or not at all. This is incredibly foolish and totally self-destructive. IRS penalties are more expensive than borrowing from any banker or even resorting to a loan shark.

Remember this: If we can't convince a bank to lend us the money we need to pay taxes, we probably do not have a source of repayment we can identify. If we are unable to repay the bank, how will we ever repay the IRS (or a loan shark, for that matter)? Think about it. Don't kid yourself.

Horror stories about the IRS could fill hundreds of volumes, so we'll only tell one. It happened to a friend. His small business faced a payday with barely enough money to make the payroll. On top of this, there were payroll tax deposits to be made. In a moment of desperation, my friend decided to pay the employees, but he delayed paying the payroll taxes and his quarterly taxes. He did not have collateral for a loan or an identifiable source of repayment, so he could not get a bank loan. He chose not to approach his shareholders for a loan or to liquidate other assets. It was the desperate choice of a weary entrepreneur and it was to be the biggest mistake of his life and his company's undoing.

Over the next few months, cash flow did not improve. More tax deposits were missed. Shareholders were not informed. No loans were obtained. The IRS contacted my friend and demanded payment. They wanted all of their money immediately. The original tax liability was under $50,000, but with penalties, interest, etc., the IRS demanded over $118,000! There were few options available to the business owner. Rather than close the business, he was forced to sell the only asset the company had, its intellectual property. The price he got was a pittance because he was desperate. The business was saved, but the owner never recovered from the emotional trauma. The "fire sale" of the company's only valuable asset left the small business with no future.

To the day he died, my friend could not discuss money without becoming physically and emotionally distressed. Some would call it post-traumatic stress syndrome. Hand him a form to fill out and he would be visibly shaken and have to sit down. Start telling him about your own financial challenges and he would become agitated and ask you to change the subject. For years, he was unable to open his mail without great emotional distress. He went long periods, often weeks at a time, when he could not open any mail at all. He totally withdrew from the pressures of the world. As a result of his ordeal, he lost his business, his home, his family, and his well-being. He ended up being emotionally disabled, unable to function in a business setting, unable to hold a job, and unable to deal with even the smallest of financial matters. He was a creative genius with technical insights that should have made him a very wealthy man. Instead, he died in poverty.

The purpose of this story is not to blame the IRS for destroying this man's ability to live a normal life. He did that himself by making a bad decision. He gave the IRS the opportunity to destroy him and it did. We cannot ignore the IRS. They will not go away. They will not forgive mistakes. I believe that IRS "penalties and interest" are intentionally exorbitant in order to discourage anyone from treating the IRS like a bank. If my friend had made a timely decision about how to manage his cash flow, his whole life would have been different.

It is important to note something. My friend's tax problems were not caused by mistakes in his tax deposits. He was using adequate payroll software, so he knew *what* he owed. He *chose* not to pay it. He did the wrong thing. He borrowed money from the IRS at extremely high rates.

Pay your taxes in full and on time. Submit accurate, quarterly reports on time. Never rely on the "generosity" of the IRS. They do not have a "form" for generosity. Never expect to have mistakes overlooked or forgiven. Never do anything that would give the IRS an excuse to shut your business. This is sound advice from many who did otherwise and paid the consequences. My friend paid the price for the rest of his life. If he had chosen otherwise, his life (and death) would have been much different.

While we're on the subject, don't pick a fight with the IRS unless you are some kind of crusader and are prepared to pay onerous penalties, including jail time. Be wary of anti-tax crusaders. There are many promoting the urban legend that tax-withholding laws are unconstitutional and that you don't need to pay taxes unless you *want* to. This is foolishness! The IRS will close your business, seize your home, confiscate your business and personal assets, and send you to prison. That's their track record. Until the IRS says you don't have to pay taxes, pay your taxes. If you don't have the cash to pay your taxes, arrange financing or liquidate whatever assets are necessary. Save your home, your cars, and your life. Don't put your life in the hands of an IRS auctioneer. Face reality.

Again, this chapter is not intended to be anti-IRS. It was carefully written to explain the real world, nothing more. This reality is well documented. Do your taxes as if the IRS were in the room, looking over your shoulder. There is no substitute for peace of mind and being able to sleep at night. This will allow you to focus on making your business succeed. *That* is what being an entrepreneur is all about.

Cost Control

What is the fastest way to improve our bottom line? Is it by increasing sales? What about reducing costs? If we generate $1 in revenue, how much of it do we get to keep? A lot of things come out of that dollar; sales commissions, payroll, the cost of goods sold, rent and overhead allocations, and on and on. In an average company, *less than five cents* on each dollar will make it to the bottom line.

If we reduce expenses by $1, how much goes to the bottom line? *All of it!* Controlling costs is the quickest way to increase profit.

Let's say that we discover a way to cut costs by $10,000, all of which goes to the bottom line. What would it take to bring $10,000 to the bottom line if we were to rely on generating new sales? If our business has a 5% net profit, it would take $200,000 in totally new sales to net $10,000 to the bottom line! (5% of $200,000 is $10,000.)

In the short term, the quickest way to increase profit is simply to cut costs. In the long run, the best strategy is to control costs while *simultaneously* building revenue. From experience, we know that building revenue takes far more time and effort than controlling costs.

It is important to emphasize that cost control is not random *cost cutting.* Cutting costs purely for the sake of increasing profitability is the strategy that causes many MBAs to run businesses into the ground. There are some costs that cannot be reduced without hurting the integrity of our business, our product, or the level of our service. It takes wisdom to know which costs are necessary and which can be safely cut.

What is the cause of most business failures? Is it because management puts in too little time, as some believe? Lots of business owners believe that if they just put in enough hours working on the things within their areas of expertise, everything else will fall into place. Such foolish optimism has caused many business failures. We address this subject in the chapter entitled *The Trap*.

Is the cause of most business failures starting with inadequate funding? Can someone honestly say they are "in business" if they try to start without having enough money, no backup income to speak of, and no foreseeable cash flow? They are kidding themselves. Would anyone just decide he is going to be a boxer and walk into the ring with the likes of Mike Tyson without adequate preparation and at least a little training? Why do people quit their jobs and start businesses without enough money to cover personal expenses for a while, never mind enough resources to fund inventory, receivables, equipment, rent, and operating expenses until cash flow is adequate? This is the formula for failure and it works every time.

I need to share only one example to prove the point. A credit manager who was also a prospective entrepreneur created a powerful algorithm to make credit decisions. It proved to be so effective that he reduced credit losses for his employer to a minimum, something like a loss of a few thousand dollars on over $1 billion in revenue. His employer worked with extremely thin margins, so credit losses could have been the difference between making and losing money. Using his algorithm, he had virtually no credit losses. As a credit manager, he was a hero.

Armed with a truly effective, simple, and valuable process, he decided to go into business for himself. He paid a programmer to write software that codified his algorithm. Unfortunately, he began to run out of money before he could even finish the software, so he gave the programmer a 1/3 ownership in the software to complete the programming. Then, instead of building his business on the side while he maintained his well-paid position with his grateful employer, he quit his job "to go into business." He gambled everything and he *lost* everything! He ran out of money almost immediately. He found himself unemployed, with no income, no savings, and no business. It was not long before he lost his home. Then, he lost his family. The only thing he didn't lose was his business because he never had a business to lose. After losing everything, depression hit him.

I knew this entrepreneur to be a good man. He had a great idea for business. He created a valuable product that no one else offered. However, he was never "in business." Like many others, he kidded himself, but reality was not fooled. I've said it before, reality is harsh and it is just as unforgiving as gravity. Ignoring reality has caused many entrepreneurs to fail before they actually got "into business."

One business term that irritates me is "cash burn rate." I define the burn rate as the rate a business *loses money* as it gambles on becoming profitable. This may work for big business, funded by other people's money, usually cash siphoned from the "public" trough, but small businesses have no such cushion. For us, it is usually "do or die!" And, far too often, it is "die!"

Back to the original question: What is the cause of most business failures? I am convinced that the reason most *operating* businesses fail (those that actually get into business) is costs getting out of control! That's right, sales are growing, people are working hard, collections may be adequate, but costs are not monitored and they get out of control. This means both the cost of goods sold and operating costs. Why? How?

Here is another reality. Most operating companies have slim margins. Any company enjoying high margins will automatically attract competitors and, over time, prices will be driven down. It's a fundamental law of economics.

Once AT&T lost its monopoly, rates began a long downward trend, along with AT&T's profits. Now, the long distance industry is struggling. Competition has pushed rates so far down some companies have declared bankruptcy. What has AT&T done? It started gobbling up smaller companies and firing their employees, thereby *reducing costs* to increase profitability. Aside from changes in technology, *competition* will always be the single most important economic factor in keeping prices down.

Given that almost all businesses eventually operate on thin margins, the surest way to succeed is to make sure all costs are kept as low as possible without tarnishing the quality of the company's product or service. We're not talking about being "cheap" or cutting corners. We're talking about keeping costs under control.

Costs get out of control a little at a time. How? Too many people doing what fewer people used to do. Too much overtime. The creeping up of cost of goods sold. The expansion of operating overhead, delivery costs, production costs, advertising, marketing, and on and on. There are as many risks as there are expense categories. So, how are costs monitored? The answer is *Cash Management*! We're back to budgeting—excuse me—I mean cash management again. We need to *constantly* compare actual results versus what was forecasted. That means both cash flow budgets and profit projections. Most accounting systems include profit projections. Few people use them. Even fewer businesses use cash flow budgeting.

We must regularly evaluate our costs to determine which of them have grown to be extraneous. One small business had a full-time front office manager who was so busy she had a helper come in once a week. When that front office manager came down with an extended illness, a temporary was hired to cover for her. The temp was a student, a hard worker, and totally honest. As she learned the tasks, she observed that the job would not be enough to keep her busy for more than a few hours a day, never mind eight hours. In only a few days, the temp completed the work that had backlogged. Then, as she learned her job better, she could finish her work in less than two hours each day and have nothing to do—nothing at all!

The interesting fact is that the permanent front office manager had "worked" in that position for years and always *looked* busy. It wasn't long after that the temp quit to take a job that would keep her busy. The vacant position was simply eliminated. So was the part time position! Coworkers assumed what duties there were, and the rest of the "work" that filled the former front office manager's day was never missed. All of the costs that were eliminated went to the bottom line.

How many positions in our company might fit this situation? Entrepreneurs get so busy building their company they do not look to see what needs to be rebuilt. Every company evolves as it grows. Some activities, like the vestigial appendix in our digestive tract, may have been useful once, but they are now obsolete. Eliminating those activities, those processes, that staff, that truck, that department, will save serious money. Remember, every dollar saved goes to the bottom line.

At one of the turn-around companies I worked with, overstaffing was a real problem, so was morale. Everyone was stressed all the time because there was never enough to do. One of the owners of the business liked to hire as many pretty girls as he could. There was nothing inappropriate in the relationships with these attractive girls, but he hired too many of them. One day, a new girl arrived at my office asking to apply for a job. I informed her that we had no openings. (At that time, we were still overstaffed.) She informed me that one of the owners of the business (the one that liked pretty girls) had instructed her to see me about a job. I excused myself and asked the owner what he had in mind for her to do. He admitted that he had nothing in particular in mind. He was just impressed with the girl's "qualifications" and he didn't want them to go to waste. He wanted me to see if there was anything she could do there. I figured that about all she could do was add to the problem.

Shortly thereafter, I had to fire one of those pretty girls for "misbehaving." What happened? Morale soared. Why? Everyone had enough work to do for a change. Everyone felt needed. No one was worried about being fired. Costs were reduced and morale was increased in a single act. Having too many employees is more than just an economic issue.

Here's a rule of thumb for you. *If your employees are not overworked, you are overstaffed.* Time after time this axiom has proven to be true. It seems that we rarely hire a half a person or a quarter of a person, but often, the tasks they are hired to do just don't require a full-time person. So, to look busy, they fill their time with make-work tasks. These useless tasks will become a permanent part of that person's daily routine and will always prevent that person from being 100% "productive." When we hire someone, we should be taking the load off enough people that we will immediately give this person a full-time job. Otherwise, their "invented" tasks will get in the way of doing real work as it becomes available.

Growth

What are the most important factors in achieving long-term success in any industry? In the last chapter we discussed the first factor, the need to control costs. The second factor is growth. Growth is not just important, it's essential to success, but, as with costs, it must be *controlled.*

In 1987, the SBA completed a 10-year study, focusing on growth (or the lack of it) as a factor in the failure rates of small businesses. Using the number of employees as the measuring stick, it became obvious that there was a positive relationship between growth and success.

We have all heard the old axiom that only one business in five will make it to five years. Many old axioms are accurate. This one is off a bit. According to this survey, only 60% of companies in all industries failed, not 80%, and it covered a six-year period, not five. This was something of a surprise, but the role played by growth was even more surprising.

If a company had no growth at all, there was a 72.5% chance of failure. Remarkably, if a company grew by as little as one to four employees, the incidence of failure dropped to 33.7%. Growing by five to nine employees dropped the failure rate to under 25%. Businesses that grew by 10 or more employees failed less than 22% of the time. Growth *is* important. It is interesting to note that this survey was completed in 1987, including the Reagan years of unequalled economic prosperity. If growth is important in a good economy, it is absolutely essential in a weak economy. The following chart tells the whole story quite eloquently.

Failure Rate

	All Classes	No Growth	Low Growth 1 to 4	Medium Growth 5 to 9	High Growth 10+
All Industries	60.2	72.5	33.7	24.5	21.6
Construction	64.7	75.9	35.0	27.8	25.7
Transportation	60.3	74.3	31.5	27.6	24.4
Manufacturing	53.1	73.0	33.1	26.5	24.0
Mining	60.9	72.9	32.2	38.5	43.0
Retail Trade	61.6	72.9	37.3	25.6	23.2
Wholesale Trade	55.7	71.7	33.5	25.1	22.8
Services	59.7	71.3	30.9	20.6	16.5
Financial Related	61.4	71.3	31.3	23.6	21.5
Agricultural	56.9	65.0	25.3	19.3	17.2

Boxed amounts are the highest failure rates in each Growth Category.
Source: US SBA, Office of Advocacy, Small Business Database
USELM File, Version 8, November 1987

Before going on with this topic, it is important to step back and point out that growth for its own sake is not good. Like a body builder who adds 50 pounds of muscle mass to his body, it becomes something that has to be maintained, fed, exercised, clothed, etc. If that muscle mass was created as a result of hard physical labor, part of a lifestyle, those muscles have a reason to exist. In business, adding an employee for the single purpose of increasing numbers brings increased payroll, space requirements, supervisory duties, etc. Adding an employee to handle increased shipping needs, to open a new location, or to handle expanded sales, means that growth is creating a need for new employees.

One entrepreneur with a string of business failures to his credit, lectured me that if I were to add several employees to A-Systems, the company's success would quickly justify them. Unfortunately, his backwards idea of "the cart before the horse" is one of the reasons he repeatedly failed in business.

Growth must have a goal, a reason, or address an *opportunity*. Adding employees should be the result a need caused by increased sales. This might seem obvious, but after lecturing in numerous settings, I have learned that *nothing* is obvious.

On the other hand, it might be said that it is obvious that growing companies add employees as a byproduct of their success. The argument might be made that the survey proves nothing. Perhaps, but there is another perspective to be considered.

Some people believe that growth actually increases risk. They believe it is best to remain as small as possible to reduce that risk. This survey proves just the opposite to be true. It is much riskier to stay stagnant. That's what we need to know. If we're not growing, we're coasting, and we can only coast downhill. We actually reduce the risk of failure if we take advantage of appropriate opportunities *and grow*.

There is a second point worth considering. We are not immune from the painful "up and down cycles" of the economy. Inevitably, there are good times and there are bad times. What happens to a business with 25 employees when times get tough? They may have to cut back, so they might lay off 5 or 10 employees. What happens if the business has been kept intentionally small and there is only one employee?

Where do we look for growth? There are two responsibilities here, marketing and sales. The marketing manager finds a way to create demand for our product or service. The sales manager is the one that directs and focuses our sales efforts and trains our staff. We need to have ultimate confidence in the insights and efforts of these two individuals. Later, we are going to explain marketing in greater depth. For now, let's just say that growth through marketing can turn a tiny company into a huge success in a big hurry. The sale of products and services, one at a time, is far less effective in creating significant growth. Sometimes, we get so excited about making *a* sale, that we ignore the opportunity to do something that will lead to *a hundred* or *a thousand* sales, per day, including weekends.

As entrepreneurs and managers of small businesses we might do well to focus our attention on seeking bigger opportunities. We should be open to opportunities that come our way and we must determine how to take advantage of them. Sometimes, our greatest opportunities may become available when we least expect them, but we must be prepared.

W. Somerset Maugham wrote a story called "The Verger." It is the story of opportunity, cloaked in crisis. A verger is something akin to a handyman or janitor in the Church of England. Whenever there is a procession down the aisle at church, the verger is the one carrying the cross. After that brief weekly assignment, he fills his time as the handyman. Traditionally, being a verger meant having a job for life. Not so in Maugham's story.

The verger at St. Peter's, Neville Square was named Albert Edward Foreman, a man who recognized an opportunity at a time when his life was in crisis. Were it not for that crisis, he would never have sought the opportunity that changed his life.

> Albert was comfortable with his job of sixteen years. Being a hard worker of high character and native intelligence, Albert's duties as verger did not suffer in any way from the fact that he could neither read nor write. In fact, Albert's work was known to be exceptional. However, a new vicar with "higher" values felt that a man in the

employ of the church must be able to read and write. Given the opportunity to learn, Albert declined. He felt he was too old a dog to learn new tricks. He was promptly sacked, dismissed, fired, canned, told to hit the road. He was no longer needed. Albert was shocked. [Warning: Managers who exercise their power to enforce petty and arbitrary rules are a threat to the success of any business. These people are tyrants or bureaucrats and they have no place in small business. They will probably prosper in big business or government environments, especially government.]

As jobless Albert left for home, he desired to indulge in a personal treat, a cigarette. Walking down the long street he was unable to fulfill his desire because there were no tobacco shops on the street. He retraced his steps to confirm that he had not missed it in his state of mind. There were definitely no cigarette shops to be found.

The next day he found a small vacant shop on that street and rented it. With the savings he had accumulated as a frugal verger, he stocked the store and added newspapers as well. His wife discouraged him, believing he had come down from being a verger, a position of some respect in the community. Albert stayed his course, knowing that times change and the church was not what it once was.

Albert's store prospered. He learned much. A year later, Albert located another long street that had no tobacco shop. He rented a spot and hired someone to manage the store. With two successful shops, Albert began to look for other streets where he might open more shops. After ten years, Albert had ten successful shops.

One day as Albert was making his weekly bank deposit, the bank manager asked to speak with him privately. Observing that Albert had amassed a considerable amount of cash, the manager suggested there was a way to invest the cash and obtain a nice return. The bank manager offered to take care of the details if Albert would sign a transfer form. Albert liked the idea, but was unsure of signing any document he could not read. Albert admitted that he could not write, except for his name, and he had only "learnt" to do that since going into business.

The manager was incredulous, saying "...do you mean to say that you've built up this important business and amassed a fortune of thirty thousand pounds without being able to read or write? Good grief, man, what would you be now if you had been able to?"

"I can tell you that, sir," he said, "I'd be verger of St. Peter's, Neville Square."

Albert Foreman turned his crisis into an opportunity and it changed his life. Growth is a viable strategy when it is the result of finding or creating an opportunity. The point to remember is that opportunities for growth must be sought out and evaluated. If Ralph Lauren had limited himself to shirts, he would not have made it to the cover of *Time Magazine* as the "600 Million Dollar Man." If Jimmy Dean had limited himself to singing country music, we wouldn't be eating his great sausage for breakfast. If Elvis had limited himself to driving a truck, he would never have become *The King*. If Einstein had been satisfied as a patent clerk, we would not be so confused about his theory of relativity.

"But," you ask, "if I do one thing and I do it well, isn't *that* the best thing for me to do?" The appropriate response is, if you do one thing well, why not do it more often, in more places, for more people? Doesn't that benefit everyone? Of course it does. What if the one thing you do well just doesn't happen to be the thing you are doing now? Maybe it's a good idea to keep an open mind. We're not talking about "chasing rainbows" here. We're talking about finding what each of us does best and doing it. The US Army calls that "Be all that you can be." It is an excellent idea.

Let me tell another story. This one is not fiction. When my sons played recreational soccer, they had a series of volunteer coaches. They were all good people. One of them was especially interesting. She was a teenager, only three years older than the boys she was coaching. She, along with a couple of her girlfriends, were doing an excellent job of teaching the boys about controlling the ball, discipline, playing their positions, etc. I was impressed. I noticed that "Coach" missed several games and practices because she was working out, trying to earn a position on the US Olympic Ski Team. She wanted to be an aerialist, one of those skiers who do incredible gymnastic feats on skis. Unfortunately, she was just a wisp of a girl, maybe five feet tall and barely over 100 pounds. She was in excellent shape and was very disciplined, but I wondered if she had the bulk necessary to flip skis around and dazzle people as an aerialist. Apparently, she wasn't going to make the cut, but she did not give up. The opportunity came for her to try a new sport for the Olympics. She tried out and made the US Olympic team. Then, she earned the first gold medal for the skeleton, in the 2002 Winter Olympics here in Salt Lake City. Her name is Tristan Gale. She took advantage of a different opportunity and made history. In business, we must keep our minds open to new opportunity.

While it is important to grow opportunities, growth must have controls. What kind of controls? Accounting controls, cash controls, cost controls, asset controls, employee controls, process controls, all kinds of controls—controls we call Standard Operating Procedures.

If we don't have control of our business, how can we sleep well at night? Do we need prescription medication or some other chemical intervention? If this is the case, it's time to reevaluate what we are doing.

There was a retailer in southern Idaho. Like Albert Foreman, he recognized the opportunity to expand by opening a second store in a nearby town and decided to do something about it. This retailer hired a manager too, but he let the manager run the new store with no controls. In his own words, he "just trusted the guy." This "guy" took advantage of his opportunities too, but the opportunities he chose were related to stealing from his employer. The branch never made money. It had to be closed at a huge loss.

Lack of management control was the cause of this failure. Oh sure, there was theft involved, but the fault was the manager's for allowing it to happen, for creating the opportunity. "But," some plead, "It wasn't really his fault." If it is necessary to blame someone else, find an excuse, or deny reality, then it was technically the employee's fault. In the real world, it was the owner's fault and in the real world the owner is the one who paid the price. Get real. Even if we don't personally make the mistakes, we are the ones that pay for them.

There is a story that the president of Sinclair Oil signs every check that leaves Sinclair Oil. This may or may not be true. This level of control may be excessive, but it makes a point. If we do not maintain control, we lose it. If we lose control, we put our business at risk. It's that simple.

Growth brings other opportunities too. Success allows us do to things we would never get to do as an average person. We all know what money can do.

There is a story, not a fable, but the actual history of two individuals. Both started in the same business at the same time. Both had retail stores in a growing metropolitan area. They were located approximately 10 blocks apart. There was nothing special about either store or either store's owner. They were quite ordinary merchants.

One owner was happy with a single store. It was profitable, provided him an adequate living, and it served the surrounding area well. By one definition, he was successful. When the owner retired, he closed the store. He left many loyal customers who were disappointed to see him and his store go. The vacant building was put on the national historic register. Nothing more remains to indicate he and his store were ever there.

The owner of the second store was also successful, but he was not as easily satisfied. He decided if he could do well with one store, he could do twice as well with two. Like the verger, he opened a second store in a new neighborhood. He was right. It did well too. One after another, he added stores in new neighborhoods. Before many years he had over 50 stores in 30 towns. In time, he decided he needed to go public and raise millions of dollars. He used that money to open new stores and buy a few competitors. Because his was a public company, he was able to buy a chain of stores in another state "for stock," then another, and another. He formed a strategic alliance with another retailer and opened a chain of stores from California to Florida. Within a few years there was a long list of stores in his chain. When the owner decided it was time to retire, he agreed to being acquired by another large chain. Over the years, he donated hundreds of millions of dollars to public and private schools, hospitals, rest homes, churches, charities, and on and on and on.

Which of these entrepreneurs would you like to be? Bear in mind that both were "successful".

SOP

For most people, SOP is the acronym for *Standard Operating Procedures*. For others, it means *Seat of Pants*. The difference is more than just a clever joke.

In 1973 while I was working for Dun & Bradstreet, I spent 310 nights on the road. It was my job to visit business owners in Idaho, interview them, and write their credit reports. When I visited contractors, I often had to go to their homes in the evening to catch them because during the day they could be anywhere, working at or supervising jobs.

One evening, I drove up to a plumber's house. He was standing in the yard watering his lawn. He was a grandfatherly type with thick, white hair and a big smile. He welcomed me to his "office" as he turned off the water and shook my hand. He had a little time to share with me, so we chatted. He informed me that there were only three things he needed to remember as a plumber. First, sewage flows down hill. Second, payday is Friday. Third, and most important, don't chew your nails. Then, he added, if you belong to the union, you don't need to wear a belt. Obviously, he didn't take himself too seriously. (That is a virtue for everyone in small business.)

After a chuckle, we got to the business at hand. In order to give him a credit rating, it was necessary for me to obtain a financial statement on his business. If a financial statement was not available, I was allowed to accept estimates from the owner. Certainly, some information was better than having nothing at all. Very few small contractors had any type of financial statement on hand, so this guy was typical and I knew what to do. I asked him a series of questions about his assets and liabilities.

I started with his accounts receivable. "How much are you owed?" I asked.

He pulled a small notebook from his overalls and flipped a few pages over. He scratched his whiskered chin and said, "About $1,200."

I wrote it down and asked how much he had in inventory.

He said, "I have a few things on that truck over there," pointing to an old white pickup that was fully equipped with toolboxes. "Maybe $200 worth."

I wrote it down and asked how much he owed on inventory and supplies.

He shook his head, "I don't owe anyone anything. I pay cash for everything." He was proud of that fact.

I understood that. Being debt free is a nice way to run a small business. I went on, asking how much his truck was worth.

We walked over to it as he evaluated it. The truck was white, but reddish-yellow rust stains streaked down the sides here and there. He laughed and said he wasn't interested in washing the truck just in case it was the rust that was holding it together. He gave me a figure that he thought it would take to replace it. It was reasonable, so I wrote it down.

I asked if he owed anything on the truck. It gave him a chance to proudly repeat that he didn't owe anyone anything.

I asked how much he had in tools and equipment. He gave me a figure that sounded a little low for a plumber, but reasonable enough, so I wrote it down.

There was only one business asset left to list. I asked him how much money he had in the bank. I usually left this question until last. When it was the first question, the interview often ended there.

He shook his head. "Not a cent." Then, he reached into the pocket of his overalls and pulled out a wad of cash and counted out $700. That was his "Cash" balance.

This plumber is typical of thousands of business owners in all lines of business. They operate by the seat of their pants: SOP! Many do it well, but one slipup and they're in trouble. Take this plumber for example. If he breaks his leg tomorrow, he's out of business for weeks. If his truck breaks down or it gets disabled in an accident, he's out of business for a while. If he gets an extended illness from the substances he is exposed to (or from chewing his nails), he's in trouble. This is the high-risk way to run a business.

It might look like we're talking about two different things, the size of the business and the method of operating the business, but they are totally interwoven. As long as he runs the business by the seat of his pants, the size of his business is limited. He may be a great guy, a wonderful plumber, and on and on, but his business strategy is self-limiting.

So, what are Standard Operating Procedures? They are the rules employees can rely on when we aren't there to tell them what to do. There are two kinds of employees we need to be careful of. First, those that won't do anything *until* we tell them and those that won't do anything *except* what we tell them. Standard Operating Procedures are not an alternative to thinking; they are guidelines for thinking. SOP provides the consistency customers expect and the control we need because SOP provides guidelines the employees need.

When I was a banker, the bank's SOP manual comprised three volumes and each was more than three inches thick. If you have ever dealt with a bank, you know they have procedures for everything. There are forms that need to be processed, applications that need to be approved, boxes that need to be checked, places that need to be initialed, and copies of everything for everyone. We had procedures for unlocking the door, for entering the vault, for counting night deposits, for approving a check, even procedures for being robbed. This may seem like overkill, but it is necessary. When bankers get creative and invent their own procedures, they are usually trying to get away with something—something like the bank's money.

Procedures may be like good fences and locks. The old expression that "good fences make good neighbors" may have some application here. It may be a bit of a stretch, but perhaps "good procedures make good employees."

When we have employees, they need to know what we expect them to do. There are two ways to do this. We can be there to supervise their work every minute or we can use standard operating procedures. For most companies, these may need to be written down. An actual book or booklet may be required. For some, a checklist of opening and closing procedures is all that will be necessary. Employees with no idea what policy, procedure, or rule of thumb to follow, will require constant supervision.

If there are no standardized operating procedures, employees have to make things up as they go. This may sound obvious, but it is not. One very human trait is the tendency to assume that because we know something and because we understand it so well, it must be equally obvious to everyone else. This is a bad assumption with potentially dire consequences.

Sometimes the best procedures we can establish are those that teach employees how to think. When I was a banker, I was taught at the "master's feet." My boss, L. Reed Wood, was called "the banker's banker" by the president of a competing bank. Not only was Reed a great banker, he was a great teacher.

As a new loan officer, I needed Reed's approval for any loan I proposed to make. Reed was an expert at asking questions. It was that talent which required me to be prepared, so I could respond intelligently when I took a loan request to him. I had to be ready with a lot of answers, so I developed an inquisitive interview technique to obtain the necessary information from loan customers. Only when I was totally prepared, would I dare present it to Reed. He never made it easy. He never once said, "Sounds like a good loan to me. Let's make it." He would always ask me what I thought. If I had missed something significant, he would ask questions in a round about way that would prompt me to figure out what I had missed. I don't ever remember him giving me instructions to "Do it this way."

He wasn't critical of me. He didn't ask me to be creative or to stop bothering him. He was logical, stimulating, positive, instructive, and encouraging. In a brief period I learned a lot. I learned how to reason it out myself. He never actually told me to figure it out for myself; he just showed me how to think it through. Years later, I learned that many of the best loan officers in the bank had worked with Reed at one time or another. It was a considered a compliment to be assigned to work for him.

What Reed taught us could not be found in any of our SOP manuals. It was, however, written on our souls. I will forever be indebted to the man who took the time to teach me how to ask good questions in order to make good decisions.

Now, let's look at the other side, the dark side of Standard Operating Procedures. The bank had "internal auditors" whose job it was to pore over every loan, review every document and every piece of collateral, looking for things that were done incorrectly. They were less than affectionately referred to as "maggots." They were the epitome of pencil-necked bureaucrats. In their minds, everything had to be done exactly by the book with no variance in any way, for any reason. Anything less was a mortal banking-sin. Unfortunately, they did not recognize that a *good* loan with less than perfect documentation was *still* a good loan. They ignored the reality that a *bad* loan with perfect documentation was *still* a bad loan. All of the documentation in the world could not change a bad loan into a good loan. They followed bank procedures mechanically, mindlessly, to the letter. Here is the parallel: Thinking is more important. Your employees need to know how to think for themselves, to reason things out while applying the *guidelines* we established as Standard Operating Procedures.

As an aside, we are now facing a generation unprepared to work. Many young people have parents who *gave* their children everything rather than teach them how to work. They have not learned to think for themselves. These are good kids, but they come to us as novice employees, who have no idea what work truly is and that responsibility falls on us.

Back to banking: This may be difficult to believe, but the bank auditors would finish an audit and literally *count* every "t" that wasn't crossed and every "i" that wasn't dotted. This is *not* an exaggeration! Their report listed every "variance" from policy and loan officers were required to immediately correct these "deficiencies" and respond in writing to the senior auditor, with a copy to the administrator over commercial lending. Wow!

Rigid enforcement of voluminous Standard Operating Procedures discourages thinking, thereby eliminating the opportunity to develop good judgment. Thinking is replaced with mechanical decision-making. Can you say, "Credit Score?" In business, SOP can be similarly overdone, especially when the focus is on the negative and *form* is stressed over *function*.

As a parting contribution when I left banking, I drafted a formal proposal and submitted it to the Senior Vice President over Commercial Lending. I suggested that instead of focusing so much attention on how many "boxes were not checked" in the review of a loan officer's portfolio, they consider evaluating what he did right. For instance, how many loans did he book? How much money did he lend? How many loans were paid on time? How many were properly documented at 95% accuracy or greater? What was his total loan portfolio? How many customers did he serve? How much income did he generate? What was his value to the bank?

Measuring an employee's contribution to the bank was a novel idea. It's a good idea for every business. Surprisingly, it struck the senior vice president of the bank in a positive way. I don't know if anything ever came of my suggestion because I left banking to accept a position that was better paid. My new position didn't have the prestige, the impressive title, or the expensive desk I enjoyed at the bank, but I was able to make enough money to afford the luxury of having children.

What does this all boil down to? Having standardized operating procedures provides a yardstick that we can use to "measure" employees. Employees can even use guidelines to measure themselves. When this happens, they require less supervision. They develop good judgment. That allows or even stimulates growth. And, as we have seen, growth reduces the risk of failure.

SWOT

What is *SWOT*? It is a *reality check.* It requires us to ask questions whose answers we may not want to hear: What are our *S*trengths, *W*eaknesses, *O*pportunities, and *T*hreats? That is SWOT. Each time a SWOT analysis is performed it has the potential to refresh and renew our business. The continued emphasis is on seeking opportunity, discovering where growth might lie, and pondering what the future might hold if we choose different strategies. It helps us to refocus on *what* we should be doing, *when* we should be doing it, and *why* we should be doing it. This process will give us "wisdom."

Doing a SWOT analysis is also a key part to preparing a business plan. Some might say, "I don't need a business plan! I know who I am and I know what I am doing." Perhaps, but we will understand what we are doing better and we can do it better, if we go through the *mental* exercise necessary to prepare a business plan. The result doesn't need to be shown to anyone. No one will "grade" it.

The 90-Minute MBA® contains three processes that combine to create much of what is needed in an insightful business plan. We covered cash forecasting, a necessary tool for all startup companies and operating companies. The next process is doing a SWOT analysis, so here are the questions that must be answered.

<u>Strengths</u>

So, what are our strengths? What makes us think we can survive in this competitive world? What makes us think we're so special? What do we have that would make a customer seek us out to give us money? Are we faster, better, cheaper, easier, more comprehensive, more durable, or more convenient? What differentiates us from the competition? What adjectives describe our business, product, or service?

What is there about our company, our collective skills or talents, staff, location, product, warehouse, website, etc. that makes us unique? What do we have to offer that cannot be found elsewhere at a better price, in higher quantities, with better quality, at a more convenient location, with friendlier staff, etc.?

If we have something unique to offer, we have a reason to be in business. If not, we should keep our day job. The old adage about building a better mousetrap "and the world will beat a path to our doorstep" isn't exactly true. If no one knows who we are, what we have, and where to find us, we are just the same as the hermit who lives in the cave in near the edge of town. You say that you didn't know there was a hermit there? He's been there for years, but no one knows about him. That's the point.

Now, I'll tell you what makes us special. We (small businesses) are the lifeblood of the US economy. For every two jobs eliminated by Fortune 500 companies (the guys who get all the press, the government bailouts, the tax breaks, and all the attention), for every two jobs they destroy, *we create eleven*! Surprised? The creativity, imagination, innovation, hard work, courage, and drive that make the US economy vital are found within the walls of small businesses. Big businesses are heavily invested in the technology and inventory of their present product lines.

Most big businesses are publicly held. They answer to shareholders on a quarterly basis. They are highly motivated by short-term results. If they discount or write-down their inventory of 10 gazillion patented "whatzits" because R&D invented a much faster version, it will result in a terrible third quarter report. The company's stock will go down in value and management will be criticized in the *Wall Street Journal.* It will look like the company doesn't know what it's doing. It's in their best interest to defend the status quo, at least for the short term. Short term, however, is how they report to shareholders and short term is how the market values their stock. Short term is what business headlines are written about. Stock prices can fluctuate wildly based on the most insignificant, short-term data. Big business often finds itself sacrificing what is best for what might positively impact the price of its stock because the market is watching. One question will make the point. Does anyone really believe that the value of a business fluctuates with every tick of the clock? If you watch stock prices, you might be deceived into thinking so. In the 1990s, we saw what the pressure to report higher profits did to public companies. Can you say, "Enron?"

Does small business have this kind of internal conflict? Sometimes, but certainly not to the degree of big business. *Small businesses exist to kick big businesses butts.* One way we do that is by making big business's inventories become obsolete, outdated, and overpriced. Does big business live in fear of what small business is going to do next? Yes, they do. We know it and we love it! Here is the reality. Big business has everything to lose. Small business has everything to gain.

How does big business respond to innovation from small business? They buy us out. They have to. Sometimes they have to buy us out to bury us until they can liquidate their huge inventory of obsolete products. Then, our new product line can replace theirs and make it look like they are geniuses.

Without mentioning the names of the guilty, I'll give an example. In the 1980s, there was a small company that created a fully integrated software package with capacities that were well beyond anything then on the market. Users were incredibly loyal because of the power built into this easy to master product. It didn't take sophisticated programming knowledge to create all kinds of interactive and linked databases, spreadsheets, and word processor applications that were powerful and foolproof. In 1985, their spreadsheet had functions that Microsoft Excel® still doesn't have over two decades later. They had *superlative* software.

As a nonprogrammer, I used that software to create an application that forecasted and tracked the financial operations of a $750 million company. There was a menu of reports available to meet the exacting needs of management for timely information. The price? That powerful software cost less than $800. It was vastly superior to anything on the market at any price and its success was growing internationally. It appeared to have a great future, but it was there one day and gone the next. The company was gone.

Rumor had it that the product was a serious threat to high-priced product lines of a *huge* public software company. The bigger company's cumbersome products cost many times more than the easy to use products of the small company. Don't be surprised, but the huge company with the high priced software was the one that bought and buried the small company. Big business has to defend the status quo because they have so much invested in it. In this case, as with many, big business protected an inferior product by the eliminating a superior product. As small business, our strength is bringing superior products and services to the market. We can act quickly.

<u>Weaknesses</u>

What is our company's weakness? Certainly, by definition, our *size* is a significant weakness. With few exceptions, the description of a small business is one that is undercapitalized. There is never enough money. In addition to being undercapitalized, what is the most vulnerable thing about our company, our product, and our staff? Answering this question may require some soul searching, but we need to be brutally honest. We cannot afford to kid ourselves. This is a difficult assignment. This is reality.

Most people live in a world of their own creation. Reality only infringes on it periodically. Then, it is quickly suppressed, ignored, and denied. As entrepreneurs, we cannot afford the luxury of living in a world of delusions. Denying reality does not change it and ignoring it will not make it go away. Abraham Lincoln asked, "*If you call a dog s tail a leg, how many legs does he have? Four. Calling it a leg doesn t make it a leg!*"

We can kid other people, but we shouldn't kid ourselves. What are our weaknesses? How badly are we under-capitalized? What are our options? Do we have the kind of people with the kinds of expertise we need? Can we afford them? Where will we find them? Can we produce a marketable product or service at a competitive price and still generate enough profit (and cash flow) to stay in business? Are we committed to making this business succeed or is it a hobby with delusions of grandeur?

Gravity exists. It doesn't care if we know about it or not. Ignoring it does not reduce its influence or its consequences. On the other hand, if we understand gravity, we might create a product that uses the effects of the moon's and the earth's gravity to create low-cost electricity. We keep hearing that "knowledge is power," and it keeps proving true.

<u>Opportunities</u>

What opportunities are out there that our competitors are not aware of? What have they overlooked in the "arrogance" that comes with their "bigness?" Let's face it; big companies act like they are stupid. They're *not* stupid, but when they defend the status quo, it often looks that way. What are our competitors doing wrong? Which of our competitor's weaknesses are addressed by our strengths? What part of our existing market is untapped? How can we get access to it? Can we do it without notifying our competitors in advance of what we are doing? What do we do well that can be applied to a totally new market? To new customers? With new services? With other complementary products? Are there new applications of our existing products or services? What are our existing customers buying from someone else that we might be able to provide? This is the kind of creative thought that sets us apart from big business.

<u>Threats</u>

This is an extension of who and what might take advantage of our weaknesses. Who is out to get us and how are they going to do it? This is a hard question. Again, most people prefer not to ask this question. They want to bury their heads in the sand. Let's visualize that for a second. We did this when we were covering embezzlement, but it bears repeating. When we stick our heads in the sand, we stick our butts in the air. That's not exactly a safe position, if you are visualizing the same picture I am.

In time, an ignored threat may turn into reality and we will be taken by surprise. Sometimes, with all the other stresses we face each day, it feels easier to ignore what is threatening us than to deal with it. It may be easier, but it is not very smart. Let's face another reality; "easy" never has been a characteristic of running a small business.

Wisdom

I like to define wisdom as a magical combination of knowledge and experience. It doesn't have to be our own experience. It can be the experience of our competitors, our teachers, even people we do not know. In fact, sometimes it is best to learn from the *mistakes* others make, so we don't have to repeat them. If we do a SWOT analysis honestly, we can gain wisdom and insights into the very reasons that justify our existence in business or the reality that we should *not* be in business. Maybe we have no justification for being in business. Maybe we have a business that could change the world. We need to do a SWOT Analysis to find out.

Business Plan

Now that you have finished a SWOT analysis, you have the backbone of a professional Business Plan. Any company without a Business Plan is like a blind bug crawling on the ground in a zebra stampede. Having a Business Plan is like being a lion watching that zebra stampede, waiting and watching, prepared for the right opportunity. The third tool for creating a valuable Business Plan is covered in the chapter called *Your Dreams*. The process of creating a Business Plan will allow powerful ideas to be crystallized. It is how we come to recognize who we are, how we fit in, and what it will take for us to succeed.

From 1983 to 1987 there was a TV series called *The A-Team.* Whenever Hannibal Smith would see his A-Team beat impossible odds and overcome unexpected obstacles, he would stick a victory cigar in the corner of his mouth, grin, and say, "Don't you love it when a plan comes together?" In business, we must have a plan. Whenever a project has been well executed, it is safe to assume that it was well planned.

The Meaning of Life

Doing a SWOT Analysis, will give us incredible insights into the meaning of our life in the world of business. In addition, it will give us the wisdom to know what we should be doing, the right things to do, if we want to succeed in business.

Employee Satisfaction

Most employers believe that money is the key to employee satisfaction. Many employees believe it is the only factor in employee satisfaction. If life were only that simple! According to the man who invented the science of "Business Management," they are wrong. Starting in the 1930s, Professor Peter F. Drucker (1909-2005) created the concepts that made business management a field of legitimate academic inquiry. He was one of the "keepers" of the insights into running a successful business. He believed there are three key issues necessary to create employee satisfaction. [As a suggestion: Any book or article by Peter F. Drucker should be studied like holy writ when it comes to business.]

The first issue Drucker listed is a *good* working environment. What does this mean? It means different things to every business. A good working environment at the sewage treatment plant is not the same as what should exist at a bank. A good working environment is not necessarily what OSHA describes, with lines and arrows on the floor. It's safe and it's as comfortable as possible, but it's more. The employer has done everything possible to make it a good place to work, given the line of business. For instance, ear protection devices are the only practical way to deal with the endless noise that baggage-handlers experience at the airport. They aren't pretty, but they are good for the people that wear them. Providing a good working environment means management knows and deals with important issues that may affect the employees, both negatively and positively.

The second issue Drucker pointed out is related to the tools the employees use. They have to be *adequate* to the job they are performing. Do they have to be state of the art? Not necessarily. For instance, if my employees “needed” state of the art computers to do their work as programmers, it would be necessary to buy new computers for everyone a couple of times a year. Every time a bigger and faster hard drive hits the market, they would need it. Every increase in processor speed would trigger another purchase. Slimmer and higher quality monitors would be required regularly and on and on. There would be no end to it.

My employees are “techies” for sure. They know what new technology is out there, but they do not expect new computers every time something new hits the market. As a matter of economic strategy when we upgrade computers, we purchase what we need from the items that were just made obsolete by the latest technology change. What this does is put us one small step behind those who must have the latest and greatest, but we do it at a fraction of the cost. As we discussed earlier, controlling costs is very important. We do it without cutting corners.

Having adequate tools means having the right tools, not necessarily the newest tools. For instance, a brand new adjustable Crescent® wrench will never take the place of a worn set of six-point sockets. A new hand truck will never be an adequate replacement for a used hydraulic pallet jack.

In this day of high technology we can easily get carried away. Does a laundromat need an Internet site? How about a dealer in rare coins? We need to keep our perspective. Remember that the ”www” in Internet addresses stands for “Wait, Wait, Wait.” When we purchase something on the Internet, chances are it will be delivered from out of state, just like in the days of mail order catalogs. It can take time, a lot of time, and we take our chances on what it will actually turn out to be when we receive it. As a matter of policy at A-Systems, we ship all software purchases the same day they are ordered. Still, certain classes of customers demand instant delivery. Others want to see and "touch" the product before buying it.

Consider yourself as the customer and what is necessary to get your business—and keep it. I buy lots of things on the Internet, especially on eBay, the world's largest garage sale. I always get it cheaper, but not necessarily faster. Sometimes what I get is nothing at all like what was promised. If your business specializes in hard to find products, the Internet is probably a wonderful place to set up shop.

Setting up a web storefront can be less expensive than renting a building, remodeling it, stocking it and advertising, but just being "on line" is no guarantee of success. I know an entrepreneur who spent $2,000 for a very colorful, professional website to sell unique, hand-carved airplane models. He never sold a single one. The dot com "boom" was a time when everyone thought there was a revolutionary new solution to an old problem. The boom was followed by the bust. Technology is great, but let's keep it in perspective. The Internet is a wonderful marketplace, but not for every product and service.

The last item necessary to create employee satisfaction is a *backlog of work*. If there is not enough work to keep everyone busy, they know it. Years ago when I was managing a small business, there were two problems that needed to be addressed. First, we had one employee who was disruptive. Her behavior portrayed a spoiled-brat attitude, a part of her personality that we couldn't change. She needed to be fired. Coincidentally, our second problem was that we did not have the cash flow to cover our staff levels. We needed to reduce costs (as covered in the chapter on Cost Control). The solution was obvious. There was some fear on the part of the owners that firing this employee would negatively impact morale. Just the opposite ended up being true. Morale soared. Why? Before that, everyone knew they were overstaffed and they knew someone had to go. They all worried who it would be. When that worry was taken away, morale skyrocketed. They felt they had job security because they were needed.

In the end, money is not *the* issue that creates employee satisfaction. If we want satisfied employees, we must work to create a good working environment, provide adequate tools, and keep a backlog of work to be done. Of course, there is an exception to every rule. In this case, the exception is the sales staff. Their income is a direct reflection of their ability and their contribution to the company. Money is a factor in their satisfaction.

I debated about whether to include this next issue. Its content, accurate or not, is clearly not politically correct. Well, the truth exists whether we like it or not, so here goes. *Men and women are different!* There, I said it! To deny it is to ignore reality. To be an effective manager, men and women *may* need to be treated differently to accommodate their different needs. We don't need to get bogged down in the debate about "glass ceilings", discrimination, different pay for the same work, etc. We do need to address the realities we must face to succeed in small business.

This story was related by someone who was a successful manager for many years. He was unusually successful in his dealings with female employees. As I talked with them, I learned that they respected him as a manager and as an individual of impeccable integrity. In fact, they all thought of him as someone that cared for them uniquely and personally. His insights are worth knowing. The story he tells follows:

One day as he walked through the office, a lady called him over to her desk. She wanted to talk about a problem. She complained about the vent that was directly above her desk. It was blowing cold air on her. She was uncomfortable. The boss looked around and saw an empty desk that didn't have an air vent above it. He suggested she move there.

The next time he walked by her desk, she was still there. Again, she called him over to her desk. Again, she complained about the cold air. This time, he suggested she have the maintenance man tape a piece of cardboard to the vent to direct the air away from her.

The next time he walked by her desk, there was no cardboard taped to the vent. Again, she called him over to her desk. Again, she complained about the cold air. This time he suggested she shut the vent off totally.

The next time he walked by her desk, the cold air was still blowing. Again, she called him over to her desk. Again, she complained about the cold air. This time he resisted the temptation to give her a solution. He stood there and talked to her for a minute. He looked her in the eye and agreed that the air was cold and she must surely be chilly. Then, he asked about something else that was happening in her life, nothing major, but it was a moment that reconnected their "personal" relationship. She thanked him for his concern and never complained about the cold air again. She regarded him as a wonderful manager. And, she was right. Listening to employees goes a long way. Communication (listening) is a necessary skill for good managers.

This wise boss once said, "When the boss whispers, it roars like a cannon." This is a warning to be careful about what we say and how it can be interpreted or misinterpreted.

One morning the manager of a business came into work, his mind overflowing with the troubling details of a complicated deal that was going bad. Millions of dollars were at risk. As he walked past the receptionist, he was considering how to get this done before the holidays, so none of his employees would have to work over Thanksgiving. He was oblivious to the receptionist as she said, "Good morning." He didn't even acknowledge her. As he walked into his office, his secretary said "Good morning" too. This time, he managed a grunt, but nothing like his usual cheerful greeting. About fifteen minutes later, there were two valuable employees in the ladies room, crying. Both thought they were about to lose their jobs. Both interpreted the boss's preoccupation as a clear communication that they were about to be fired. When the boss whispers, it roars like a cannon. Someone called this one of the "unspoken" rules of business.

A final bit of perspective that will help us deal with employees. They are not slaves. There *was* a time, in the days before labor unions, worker's rights laws, etc., when employees were little more than slaves. My family worked in the coal mines during the 1920s and 1930s. They were one level above slaves, some days, one level below them. Fortunately for everyone, that time has passed.

If you want to succeed as a manager of people in these times, a different perspective will serve you better. Think of employees as *volunteers*. They don't need to be there. They want more than a paycheck. They want to be fulfilled, to feel needed, and to feel productive. They need to be thanked for their contribution. They need to know they are a valuable part of the business. They need to know that what they are doing is adding to the world. According to the hierarchy of human needs suggested by Abraham Maslow (1908-1970), a pat on the back may be worth more than a raise. Because of the times in which we live, a literal "pat on the back" might give someone an excuse to file charges of sexual harassment, but acknowledging a job well done is essential to a *fulfilled* employee.

Counseling an Employee

Every employer has an employee who needs a little "counseling" from time to time. The reasons are as many as there are employees *and* employers. A simple, effective strategy is one that gets employees to accept responsibility for their own actions *and* the consequences of those actions. After accepting the reality that *they* are in charge of *their* own behavior, the next step is to get *them* to figure out what *they* need to do to resolve the problems *they* are causing. This technique is based on "Reality Therapy" techniques developed by the legendary psychiatrist, Dr. William Glasser, in the 1960s to deal with institutionalized patients. It is equally useful when applied to individuals living outside of institutional environments, those of us in the "real world."

In our example we will be interviewing Neville, an employee who is our personnel manager. Neville has a habit of *not* returning phone calls. This scenario recounts an actual event, but we won't disclose real names.

Employees throughout the company are complaining that we need to replace Neville with "someone who would be there" to support supervisors and care about our employees' needs. Actually, Neville is very supportive, he does care, and he is very competent. He just doesn't return phone calls. Neville has not evaluated his behavior, so he doesn't see it as a problem. Our responsibility, as Neville's manager, is to address the issue in such a way that we don't lose Neville as an employee, but we get him to change his ways.

The process is simple. The steps are broken down as follows:

1. Interview Neville in a "non-threatening" environment. That means not sitting behind our desk or standing over his desk when we talk to him. It means sitting face to face with him, perhaps over lunch, possibly even out of our office. We should pick a spot where the trappings and authority of our position are not part of the environment. This creates a neutral environment where we are an "equal" to Neville.
2. Get Neville to define the problem. After exchanging pleasantries and asking how Neville feels about the duties he is carrying, we can focus on the specific behavior needing to be addressed. We will probably need to ask a very pointed question to get things focused. For instance, we might ask, "*Neville, do you find it difficult to return all the calls you receive every day?*" The question cannot be accusatory or threatening. It should be based on the employee's perspective, asking for a statement of fact. If Neville does not respond by describing the problem we want to address, we need to ask increasingly focused questions until he does.

   Neville, do you receive a lot of phone calls every day?

   Do you receive so many calls that you cannot answer all of them as they come in?

   Do you have to make a lot of return calls?

   Are you able to return all of them?

   Is it difficult to return that many calls on a timely basis?

   Are there times when phone calls have to be returned the next day?

These sample questions are intended to show how to "beat around the bush" a bit. This may take a bit of practice and a generous amount of tact. If he absolutely refuses to talk about the issue, he may be denying it or avoiding the subject, so we may need to be a little blunt. With some people we may need to be very blunt. This, of course, is the last resort.

3. After he defines the problem, we must get him to describe the consequences of his behavior. For instance, we might wonder, "*Neville, what kinds of problems seem to arise when employees don t have your expertise to rely on?*" Again, the question is not accusing Neville of anything. It asks his opinion of his value (and the consequences of his behavior.) The reflection on Neville is positive, stressing his value to the company. This is usually an easier question to get the response you are seeking. People like to assure us that they are a valuable part of our business.
4 After Neville clearly expresses his understanding of the consequences of his behavior and that he *is* a valuable part of this equation, we must get him to describe the solution to the problem. We might ask straight out, "*Neville, what do you think is the solution to this problem?*" or *What do you think is the best way to deal with this?* Again, we are asking *his* opinion. The answer we seek is for him to do his part in solving the problem.
5. After Neville describes the solution we believe to be best, we must get him to evaluate his ability to do what is necessary. We might ask, "*Neville,*

can you do that?" Sometimes, the answer might be, "*No. I simply have too much to do. I have way too many things to handle to do them all the way they need to be done.*" In this case, the solution may be to hire more help or share some of his responsibilities with coworkers. Quite often, jobs have a way of getting bigger than people, especially in smaller or growing companies. If he cannot handle the job any longer, we have to consider what can be done to reallocate responsibilities or provide help. If Neville *can* do what is necessary, we are ready for the final question.

6. That final question is, *Neville, will you do that?* This is all we will need from most people. Most people do their best to keep their word. Most valuable employees like to impress their bosses. Those are the employees we want to keep. They are responsible, conscientious, diligent, and hardworking. When such an employee commits to do something, it will usually get done. Of course, there is a "class" of employees who can never be described as anything like responsible conscientious, diligent, or hardworking. As far as I know, *there is no cure for laziness!*
7. Finally, after a time, we must allow Neville to report his progress. There is nothing more satisfying to an employee than to report to the boss that a job has been completed properly. There is great fulfillment in telling the boss, "*I did my job well!*" Of course, we must acknowledge Neville's effort and the benefits created by his new behavior. Let me repeat that,

we must reward the behavior we want. That is the behavior that will be repeated. This is Psychology 101.

These steps are simple, logical, and they work. They can be amended as needed. Remember, it's not the process; it's the results that count. That doesn't mean that the end justifies the means. It means that going through the process is not the goal. Getting the behavior changed is the goal. Some interviews will find the employee describing the problem, the consequences, and the solution in the same breath: "*Sometimes I get so busy, I don t return calls fast enough. By the time I get to them, little situations have turned into big problems. I need to return my calls better. It s that simple.*" What more can we add except to ask, "*Will you do that?*"

How do we track an employee's progress? We need some way to quantify what they are doing. If we cannot measure an aspect of their work, it cannot be evaluated. The way we *feel* about an employee or they way they *feel* about what they are doing cannot be measured. Interviewing employees is a powerful method of bringing problems and solutions to an employee's awareness. Measurement is part of the process we must use as a manager. The steps in this interview process are one *suggested* method. They can be adjusted as much and as often as necessary.

Note to parents: This process works very well with children too, even younger children. Children naturally wish to please their parents. They want to be loved. This is not to suggest that parental love should be conditional. It makes the point that children (like employees) need consistency in rules, standards, and goals. Without it, they drift. They look for anyone or anything that will show them how they ought to behave and sometimes to explain "why". It takes *parents* to raise a child. If parents do not accept their responsibility, someone else will step in, perhaps “the village” or possibly a gang. If you love your kids, and believe in the politically incorrect concepts of right and wrong, individual responsibility, and personal accountability, you can use this interviewing strategy to teach them.

Hiring

Do you know how to hire an employee? Let's face it; few entrepreneurs do a good job of hiring. We get so carried away trying to convince a potential employee to work for us that we skip over the part where we determine if we actually *want* that employee. We are so used to selling our company or the product and service we provide, that instead of *interviewing* a potential employee, we try to *sell* them on working for us.

The questions that need to be answered are whether the employee fits the job, fits the company, and fits with the other employees. Unfortunately, there is no list of questions to ask *all* prospective employees to fill *all* positions in *all* companies. Wearing the hat of personnel managers, we must have a good idea of what skills, talents, and personality each job requires, and we must find out if each potential employee is a *fit*!

How do we do that? We must ask questions, be observant, and be careful. The first rule is to never hire an employee on the first interview. We just can't learn enough the first time we meet someone. It's said that 85% of our first impressions are right, but when we hire someone, we are preparing to *invest* a ton of money and time in them. We need to be more than 85% right.

Any potential employee should be interviewed by at least three different people. Each one will have a different perspective. For instance, we interview them, their prospective supervisor interviews them, and finally they spend time with their potential coworkers and they "interview" them. If a prospective employee passes all three interviews, then we can interview them again to discuss *the job* in greater detail. We have to be careful of "professional" candidates. They sound good, but this impression could be nothing more than smoke and mirrors. They could be totally lazy. They might know the right things to *say*, but have no idea what they should actually *do*.

After the interviews and discussions are done and the decision is ready to be made, ask prospective employees to describe a typical day of work, the tasks they will be performing, the philosophy behind what they are doing, and how their work fits into the company's overall goals. If they give good answers, they are looking for more than a job. They will become a contributing part of the company.

The old story about the bricklayers is appropriate here. Two men were working on a scaffold, laying bricks. The first one was asked what he was doing. He responded that he was laying bricks. The second was asked what he was doing. He said, "I'm building a skyscraper." Obviously, the second bricklayer has the vision that makes him a great employee. He is the one that will put out the extra effort to make sure the mortar is exactly right and every brick is level and in line. He is the one that will clean up his work and his work area. He will put out the extra effort to do a superior job. He will be the first one to earn a raise. He is the one that will become a good leader, leading by example.

Finally, it is a good idea to interview three people for the job. That means three people, interviewed three times, by three people. This "Rule of Threes" is adapted from the work of Brian Tracy. His seminars provide great insights into leadership, sales, and management.

Because of a whole set of laws intended to prevent discrimination, we might feel that we can't ask probing questions. May I suggest one magic phrase that is not illegal and could be used with every prospective employee? It is, "Tell me about yourself." If they ask, "What do you want to know?" Respond that, "I want to know everything you want me to know that will make me want to hire you." That may include their qualifications, their experience, their education, their talents, and their ambitions. We can see a person's race, weight, physical handicaps, and height, but these are *not* the issue. The things we can't see are the problem. The questions we are trying to answer for ourselves is whether this person can do the job and will they "fit" into our company. By doing so, we increase our chances of success. Doing anything less may be charitable, politically correct, or generous on our part, but it is not in the best interest of our company. The laws of the land change with the wind, but the laws of success dictate that we determine if we are hiring the best employee for the job.

Here are a few rules of thumb to remember. Never hire anyone you can't fire. The consequences are obvious. Never depend on the undependable or rely on the unreliable.

Banking

Do we need or do we have a borrowing relationship with a bank? If we do, we need to have a relationship with *two banks*!

The first time I said this to a banker, he literally choked. After he recovered and spent a few seconds in thought, he stumbled over the words as he repeated them and then he said, "By golly, you're right."

That's right, he said, "By golly."

The concept was new to him. He was thinking of the banker-borrower relationship from the banker's perspective. When he understood that I was addressing entrepreneurs, he reevaluated his position and agreed wholeheartedly.

I have a lot of respect for bankers, commercial bankers specifically. It is their job to gather information and make decisions. They must decide whom to trust and then express that decision in dollars and cents by making a loan. They are literally making short-term investments in their customers. It takes an unusual person to be a banker, to accept that much risk with so many people and still be able to sleep at night. As a general rule with many exceptions, commercial bankers are often the most open-minded, best educated, and the wisest people in business. Of course, there are morons and spineless bureaucrats in commercial banking just like any business, but I personally would not grace them with the honored title of "Banker."

So, let's get back to the original proposition. Why do we need two? The logic is simple. Banks change. Bankers change. Times change. We change. Further, banks are actually "comforted" by the presence of another bank. It confirms in their mind that they are dealing with a "good" customer. When they have a customer all to themselves, they might wonder if they are dealing with a flake that no one else would touch. That's when they lose sleep.

So, given the above, why do we need *two* bankers? Let me demonstrate with a story.

There is a published author who writes about business. He claims to be a marketing wizard. He owns a relatively small company that has to compete with the "big guys." He succeeds because of his marketing expertise. When I read his first book, I was impressed with his insights. At the end of the book he invited readers to submit suggestions. Well, I outlined my thoughts on dealing with bankers, the ones I'm sharing here, and mailed them off. He sent me a classy little tie tack as a "thank you" for my contribution and I heard nothing more for a year or so. One day, I received a call from a man who had been in my MBA group at college. He was calling from an airplane, reading a book that included my suggestion, word for word. It was even credited to me. At the end of my suggestion, the author zinged me by telling me to "*dance with the one what brung you*" or some slang expression to that effect. (I never bothered to read his book.)

Here was my name in national print, to be there forever, in libraries everywhere, being scolded by someone with a good reputation in the business community. I didn't mind being teased a bit, but his comment was off the mark. Its sting was in its permanence of form. Calls continued to come in from people who enjoyed giving me a bad time about what the book said, so I decided to write the author a letter. I let him know that he was dead wrong about this. I didn't ask for an apology or threaten to sue him for libel. I just wanted him to know he was as wrong as he could be.

It took several months, but I eventually got a response. After he finished his latest book tour, he sent me a copy of his new book and a brief letter. He acknowledged, in his own words, "Your words of wisdom are well taken." He went on to say, "I did learn my lesson." It seems that he had a relationship with only one bank. After a series of stellar years, he had a single down year, one in a row. He didn't lose money, but it was just not a great year. In reality, his industry was consolidating and he was one of the survivors. That meant he had less competition and therefore, an even brighter future than before. Some narrow-minded bureaucrat with influence over the bank's loan strategy had decided to withdraw from lending to that industry, not just the customer, but from the whole industry. That meant our author/businessman's line of credit was called due. He found himself "on the street, hat in hand," trying to find a new lender and explain why his last bank had booted him out. It was *not* a good situation. It could have been avoided. It should have been avoided. If he had been dealing with two banks instead of one, he would never have found himself in this kind of fix. If we need one bank, we need two.

So, how do we do this? Keep our operating account at one bank and our payroll account at another. That's simple. If we need one line of credit, we need to get a matching one at the second bank. If they insist on collateral, offer one of the banks our inventory and offer the other one our accounts receivable. If we finance equipment purchases, do some at each bank. Of course, they will both want our personal guarantees, birth certificates of our first-born children, and the keys to our homes, cars, and safe deposit boxes. This is nothing personal. It is the legacy of government intervention, protecting bankers from themselves.

How will our bankers respond when they find we have "someone else on the side?" Some of them might be a little insulted. After all, they consider us to be "their" customer. In truth, we are. We have established a relationship with a banker, not the bank. It *is* a personal relationship built upon mutual trust.

So, how do they feel about us having a relationship with the competition? First, whether they will admit it or not, they appreciate the fact that a second banker shares the opinion that our company is (or will be) a good customer. Second, they try to find ways to serve us better than the other bank. That is, if we have a conscientious banker, we might even get better service.

Why do they do this? Contrary to public opinion, bankers do not make big money on checking accounts. Their huge depositary operations are often a breakeven proposition for banks. Banks make money from loans, interest income, loan fees, etc. What they charge us for our checking account is intended to cover the cost of operations. The real "bottom-line" at the bank comes from lending money to commercial and retail customers. That means they *want* us to borrow money from them. They *need* our business. We are the ones that generate their profits.

Now, imagine that you are a banker, a commercial loan officer. You are comfortable in a gray, three-piece suit working behind an expensive desk in an upscale building. One of your customers informs you that he has an account with one of your competitors. Now, you are aware that the color of your money is *the same* as the color of the money at that other bank. What differentiates one bank from another is the way they treat their customers. As a banker, you want your customer to finance his equipment purchases with you and to use your line of credit liberally. After all, that's how you make money. Your annual review is coming up and you want to be able to brag about your "business development" efforts and your success at "account retention." You call the marketing department and arrange to get four tickets to the next NBA game in your city. You call this customer and invite him and his wife to go to the game with you. You want to create a direct relationship with him. When you find out he's available, you ask if he'd like to meet you at an expensive restaurant before the game too. He checks with his wife to make sure her schedule is clear and the night is planned.

Now, let's change places for a minute. As a bank customer, aren't you tired of kissing your banker's behind all the time, jumping through hoops to please him and his invisible "loan committee?" Wouldn't it be nicer if he spent a little time "kissing up" to you for a change? Competition is a wonderful thing. It makes us more valuable to our banker. It also allows us to turn the tables on them. This is not a matter of rubbing their nose in the competition's mess, it is just a matter of letting them know you appreciate being taken care of. When your banker gets the message, you *will be* better taken care of: tickets to a few NBA games, lunch in the bank's executive dining room, a nice package from the bank at Christmas. There are things your banker can do to let you know he appreciates your business. It's a nice feeling. You deserve it.

As I prepared this book for publication, *one* of my banks came to my office to solicit more of my business. There were three, well-dressed bankers sitting in my office *asking* for my business. When I opened my account with them, I told them I had accounts at other banks. After watching the activity in my accounts at their bank, they decided to come to my office. They asked me to apply for a line of credit or to finance equipment purchases with them. That's what we want as entrepreneurs, banks coming to our office to ask for our business.

Now, here's a word of advice about how to approach our banker for a loan. Let's start with a real experience, which shows how *not* to impress a banker.

When I was a banker, a business owner came to my desk looking disheveled and stressed. He told me that he needed "*...$50,000 that afternoon or he would go out of business*." My first response was an empathetic one. I felt an obligation to immediately help this desperate man. I was being emotional not logical. It was not an appropriate response for a banker. When I explained the situation to my boss, the wise old banker, L. Reed Wood, and asked his opinion, his insights were penetrating. As usual, he leaned back in his chair, interlaced his fingers, and rested his hands on the back of his head. After a moment of contemplation, he answered my question with a question, "*If that s how he handles his money, do you think he will handle the bank s money any better*?" Reed was right. Could it be any clearer than this? This guy was running his business by the seat of his pants. Sooner or later, failure was inevitable. Anyone that got himself into such a desperate situation was not a good risk for a bank. In my mind, I rephrased Reed's question as, *Should he lose his money and the bank s money or should he just lose his money?* I couldn't help the man. Sorry.

Compare that loan request to this one. A customer wearing a conservative suit and a nice tie enters the banker's office. He is on time for his *appointment*. He carries a nice briefcase with him. It contains a folder with financial statements and tax returns for the prior three years. He has a personal financial statement. He also has an interim statement showing year-to-date results, current through the end of last month. He introduces himself, indicating that he has an established depository relationship with the bank, a positive relationship. We later find that he has no record of bounced checks and hc carries a nice balance with the bank.

The customer describes the company, tells its history, and explains its strengths, adding pertinent information about his background. He explains that *in the future* he will need $100,000 and he wanted to make arrangements in advance. The need will not occur for six weeks when he will need to make a large seasonal inventory purchase (or pay a huge tax, make a balloon payment, make a one-time contribution to the retirement fund, etc.) He explains that he will repay the loan in 90-120 days from the early sale of seasonal inventory (or tax credits which will result in a refund, refinancing his real estate with a long-term mortgage, equity coming from the ESOP, etc.) After hearing his insights into his future cash flow, we suspect he might be using cash management techniques such as those we discussed earlier. He answers the loan officer's questions and offers his financial information after the bank indicates an interest in discussing the loan. He finishes the interview by asking the commercial loan officer to contact him *when the loan is approved.*

He is not desperate nor is he begging. He is negotiating a business relationship and has just asked the banker to do his part. He portrayed an image of confidence and competence. He made the banker feel comfortable with him. Isn't that "the beginning of a wonderful friendship?"

Now, it's important to understand how banks work. Every loan officer has an assigned lending authority, a "credit limit" of sorts, a dollar amount that a loan officer can lend without having anyone else's permission. It is based on their reputation and standing within the bank. For some it's enough to finance a used car, a very used car. For others, it's enough to buy a small country. In most banks, a committee must pass on every loan over a certain dollar amount. In other banks, loan officers are little more than documentation clerks or loan interviewers. We want to deal with someone who has an adequate lending authority for our needs. First, they can handle our smaller needs personally and second, their standing within the bank means they will have more credibility should they need the approval of a committee for our loan request.

If we are dealing with someone who has absolutely no lending authority, the actual decision on our loan must be made somewhere else, by someone we may never meet. That may be okay for the mortgage on our home, but not for our business. If we are dealing with a documentation clerk and not a loan officer, we should find a real loan officer or another bank and do business with them. If all we are dealing with is the puppet of a committee, we have no relationship. We need an advocate not a bureaucrat. If we are dealing with a bank that does not grant lending limits to loan officers, that is not a bank concerned about a business relationship with us. It is a bureaucracy concerned only with protecting itself. We want to do business with a banker, not a bureaucracy. Know that there is a difference.

If we find ourselves struggling to accommodate endless demands of the bank for more documentation, inconvenient meeting times or places, or never being able to talk to someone with decision-making authority, we can make better use of our time by finding a *real* bank. After all, we work with vendors that accommodate our needs. Why should a bank be any different? If they want our business, they should prove it. We are not an inconvenience to any bank. They make money from us. Without us, they go out of business. We are important to their success.

I'm not suggesting banks have no right to document their loans or to interrogate us in great depth about our businesses. Certainly, we are borrowing *their* money, so *they* set the terms. It's just that some banks make it very difficult to deal with them. We provide the documents they ask for, then they want more. We prepare those, then they want something else. We deliver what they asked for, then they want to arrange a meeting to discuss additional requirements. After everything seems to be set, we are asked to meet with someone at a different office. If we have this kind of experience, they are giving us a clue. They are telling us, "*We don t know what we re doing here!*" Should they do this, we need to find a real banker. Then, we need to find a second real banker and establish relationships with both of them.

When I was a banker, one of my customers said, "*Every bank s money is the same color. You are the one that makes the difference. I didn t come here to do business with this bank. I came here to do business with you.*" Later, when I left banking, my customer left the bank to find a banker that took care of him like I did. He left because my successor did not provide the level of service he expected. Too many bank customers are satisfied with bad service. Don't be one of them.

While we're talking about banks, I need to share some banker's "new math" with you. Here's the question: *When is 2% greater than 10%?* The answer is that 2% is greater when it is 2% per event and the 10% is per annum. What does that mean? It means that you can borrow money to make money. I rarely recommend debt, but there are times when borrowing money makes sense (no pun intended).

I was visiting with the owner of a men's furnishings store in Burley, Idaho. We were discussing his cash flow problems. It seemed that he was short about $100,000 for about two weeks, every month. His strategy was to stall his suppliers while still trying to maintain a good credit reputation with them. He explained that he would send the check to Company A that was payable to Company B and vice versa, or he would send checks to everyone, but "forget" to sign them. This bought him two weeks while his cash flow caught up with his accounts payable. His suppliers were not deceived. They knew a stall when they saw it and they reported his payment history as "Past due 15 days." It wasn't a terrible credit rating, but it wasn't as good as it could be.

That was *not* the real problem! In the clothing industry, it's traditional for vendors to offer retailers generous discounts for paying early. At that time, the *average* discount was around 5% if the account was paid in 10 days, or the full amount had to be paid in 30 days (5% 10, net 30 day terms). Some of his vendors even offered 8% discounts! He was missing *all* of his discounts, which was very costly. From our earlier chapter, we recognize that he was *not* doing all he could to control costs, in his case, the cost of goods sold.

It didn't sit well with me, so I pondered his situation as I drove to the next town to continue writing credit reports. I figured that if this retailer would borrow $100,000 and have it outstanding all the time (which he didn't need to do), he would pay $10,000 in interest over a year (10% of $100,000). The flip side is that if he took an average 5% discount on $100,000 every month, month after month, he would reduce his Cost of Goods Sold by $60,000 during the year ($5,000 times 12 months). This would increase his Net Profit by $50,000 ($60,000 in discount "income" minus the $10,000 in interest expense). The numbers were there. He had told me that his business only made $15,000 that year. If he followed my plan, he would increase his profit by $50,000, to over four times what he made the prior year.

I wrote the guy a letter and laid out my suggestion. I hoped to get a response, just in case I had missed something, but I never heard back from him. Of course, I was on the road 310 nights that year, so he would have had difficulty in tracking me down. Nearly a year later, he actually sent a letter to my supervisor in Salt Lake City to thank him. He said that my suggestion justified his decision to stay in business. He said that he had a record year and he owed it me. At the end of the year, he reported that he made over $65,000, a record for his store. That was 1973, so it was a tidy sum. A couple of years like that and he would not need to borrow any longer.

Borrowing money was a tool (a lever) for this entrepreneur. That is significantly different from borrowing money as a *crutch*. Too many business owners are borrowing money to "get by" when borrowing is better justified to "leverage" profitability. Typically, if we are borrowing money to *get by* what we need is equity, not a loan.

One last thought on bankers before we move on. I was the controller of a specialty food wholesaler. Our margins were tremendous and so was our market share, but the size of our specialty market was limited. In order to increase our bottom line, we acquired a line of generic food items. It was a nice complement to our specialty line and it fit well into our distribution channel, but the margins were not nearly as good as our primary product line. Our annual report showed us with a hefty jump in revenue and a nice increase in profits, but we had a lower *margin* or profit percentage. The "intellectuals" at our bank wanted us to justify the decline in our margins and lay out a plan to restore them to their prior level. My response was that our goal was "*...to bring dollars to the bottom line, not percentages. Our acquisition increased our bottom line, but if percentages were required to maintain our line of credit with your bank, we could consider selling the new subsidiary and restoring our percentages. Of course, that would reduce our net profit too.*" The bank's response was quick and conciliatory: "*Never mind! You are doing the right thing.*" Remember this, we cannot take percentages to the bank, only dollars. Here's a second thought, not *all* bankers are smart. You want two who are.

Before we move on to the next subject, there is another professional we sometimes have to deal with. I don't want to give them their own chapter, but they need to be considered.

How do we choose a lawyer? Here's the bottom line. Hiring a lawyer is *not* like finding the lowest price on getting our tires rotated. We need the best legal team we can find. If we cut corners and lose, why bother? Coming in second in litigation is like coming in second in a gunfight. If we have to do battle in court, we must win. We need the most talent, experience, and power we can *find*. Saving money on an attorney is false economy. Bungling attorneys may win cases on TV, but not in real life.

Here's the second point. Don't leave the outcome to a judge or a jury. Attorneys will tell us, "The law is what the judge ate for breakfast." That means it does not matter what the statute is, nor does it matter what the facts are, the decision of a judge can be based on anything, even something as unrelated as "what the judge had for breakfast." And, a jury trial is even worse. The best strategy, winning or losing, is to negotiate a settlement. It may take us several weeks of pretrial motions and meetings in court, but we should take control of the outcome by negotiating a settlement before the actual trial. When it becomes apparent that we may actually win, we can offer the other side a reasonable way out and end the bloodletting known as "legal fees." If we are losing, we should make an offer that will get the case settled as quickly and as cheaply as possible. This is how to deal with reality.

Customer Satisfaction

When I present this concept in seminars, I happily guarantee those in attendance that if they will listen carefully and apply what they learn, it will *change* their lives. This is not an idle boast. If you will make the effort to see how this applies to you in your business and your personal life, you will see the world differently. As a natural consequence, you will behave differently. As a result, you will get different results.

The concept I want to share is something that will redefine our businesses and our lives. It will give us a totally different perspective on our employees, our customers, our vendors, and our bankers. It even helps us with our spouses, children, etc. In short, it *can* change our lives.

Having said that, you might expect something mysterious. The truth is that this is something most of us know at an intuitive level, but we have never consciously acknowledged.

During the 1950s and the 1960s, a psychologist named Frederick Herzberg (1923-2000) came up with something he named the "Motivation-Hygiene Theory," to explain the factors that create employee satisfaction. Herzberg was a specialist in employee motivation in the workplace. I believe Herzberg's insights have application beyond the workplace, to people in general, especially to customers. Herzberg came up with a list of factors which either "satisfied" or "dissatisfied" employees. Following Herzberg's pattern, we are going to refer to situations and factors as "satisfiers" and "dissatisfiers," but we are going to apply them in a far broader way than he contemplated.

To start, let's define a satisfier as something that when it exists, we are satisfied. For our purposes, we are going to assign satisfiers a positive mathematical value. On the other hand, a dissatisfier is something that if it exists, we are dissatisfied. Following the same logic, we are going to assign dissatisfiers a negative mathematical value. That seems simple enough, but we'll need a little more explanation to understand what these words and values mean and how they affect us.

Let's say that one winter morning you arrive at work and freshly fallen snow blocks the sidewalk leading to the building. After trudging through the snow, getting it in your shoes, you know it is going to be a bad day. As you walk into the office you immediately notice that the office is frigid. The heat was off overnight. Your worn chair leans to the side and is uncomfortable. The arm is broken, allowing it to bend back and forth. The letter "M" on the keyboard of your computer keeps getting stuck. The coffee machine is broken, the vending machine only has grapefruit juice and you think grapefruit juice tastes like battery acid. You are totally *dissatisfied* this morning. Everything you have experienced has a negative mathematical value.

The next day when you arrive at work, the snow has been shoveled so you have easy access to the sidewalk. As you enter the office, you are warmed by the fresh air blowing from the vent. You sit in a comfortable chair that is in good repair and you login to the network. The computer loads your program and you are ready for work. A few minutes later you visit the lunchroom where you choose between buying hot coffee and several types of fruit juice. Are you dissatisfied? No. Are you satisfied? No. Now, wait a minute! Everything is different, actually much better, so why are you not satisfied? When all of the negatives of the previous day were removed, we ended up with a mathematical value of zero.

The third day when you arrive at work, another winter storm has clogged the roads making your drive to work akin to a near-death experience. Someone is spreading an environmentally friendly snow-melter on the freshly shoveled sidewalk in an attempt to give you a safe path. You nod to the guy pushing the spreader. You think to yourself how pleased you are that *you* work indoors. As you enter the office there is a hand-lettered sign directing all employees to the lunchroom. There you find a large box filled with all kinds of doughnuts, Danish, and fresh baked treats. A basket of fruit is there for the health-conscious employees. The counter has a sign indicating free coffee and juice this morning. Your employer knew it took something special to come in today, with the blizzard and all. You are rewarded for your extra effort with a thoughtful, but inexpensive gesture. They do care about you after all. Are you *satisfied*? You know it. Today, you were treated with satisfiers, each with positive mathematical values.

Dissatisfiers are things we hope never to encounter. When we run into a dissatisfier, it gets us down. If we never experience one, it's no big deal. After all, dissatisfiers are the way things should *not* be. Someone who experiences a total absence of dissatisfiers might say, "*There s no reason to get excited about things being the way they should be for a change.*" Take away all the dissatisfiers and we are not satisfied in the least.

Satisfiers, on the other hand, are pleasant surprises—things we don't expect, but we notice and appreciate. When we receive a satisfier, we are lifted up. And, it doesn't take that much.

Let's consider the math here. An office temperature where you can see your breath would be a big dissatisfier, say with a value of -9. A broken coffee machine might have a value of a –5. (For some, it might be a –50. It's relative.) If we eliminate all of the dissatisfiers in our environment we will never reach a level of satisfaction above zero. If we fix everything for everybody, it adds up to *nothing*! This will come as a shock to the repairman. His job description is to remove the negatives, the dissatisfiers.

Only satisfiers have a positive value. Satisfiers move us from "neutral" to "happy" territory. In our story, free coffee and fresh baked goodies on a cold, winter day might have a value of +5. Giving an employee a gift certificate for a meal at a nice restaurant might have a value of +9. A cash bonus for the same dollar amount might have a value of +1 or less. Small cash gifts tend to be "invisible" satisfiers. The cash might end up as part of our next fill-up at the gas station or disappear into our checking account, totally removed from our awareness.

Providing the same gift certificate over and over will diminish its value. One day, if it is not given, it will become a dissatisfier. When it becomes expected, it is no longer a satisfier.

Knowing the difference between satisfiers and dissatisfiers and actually applying this insight will change our lives. This guarantee is in writing. It goes into effect as soon as we *eliminate* dissatisfiers and surround our customers and our employees with satisfiers. We are guaranteed to see a difference. If we don't see a difference, we have *by definition* confused satisfiers with dissatisfiers.

Shortly after I acquired A-Systems, we shipped an update to our customers. Our senior programmer had reworked a major module in our accounting software and had fixed virtually every bug our customers had reported. It took a supreme effort on his part to complete this huge project. From his perspective, it was nearly a "miracle" in programming. Unfortunately, he was focused exclusively on the complaints our Technical Support Department had received. He believed he could make customers "happy" by eliminating all of the things that bothered them. The documentation that accompanies the update listed all of the fixes he had worked so hard to complete. It truly was an impressive list, but when the update was received, customers acted like nothing had happened! We received no phone calls, no faxes, no emails, nothing. The programmer was deeply insulted. It hurt him that our customers didn't appreciate what he had done for them. Because we know the difference between satisfiers and dissatisfiers, we know that all he did was to remove dissatisfiers. We also know that their satisfaction level went from a negative to zero. Unfortunately, he was so upset with their apparent indifference to his effort that he flatly refused to discuss its implications.

The next update included more bug fixes (a never-ending effort in the software business) and a couple of small enhancements, but this time I insisted that our programmer add a small enhancement I personally wanted in the software. The new function was a little thing that would make our customer's lives a bit easier by reducing the stress involved in printing checks. It took him less than a day to program and test. The programmer dismissed the value of this new function because he was certain it was "just a frill." He correctly pointed out that what the customers *needed* were the fixes he sent earlier. He was right, but it did not matter. What they *needed* and what they *wanted* were two different things. It was the difference between dissatisfiers and satisfiers. He refused to accept the concept.

The response to my relatively minor timesaving convenience was immediate and overwhelmingly positive. Faxes came in and customers called to gush over the wonderful “new feature.” We might have even received a fruit basket from someone. Our customers were very, very grateful for this tiny satisfier. The programmer felt even worse, almost resentful.

What our customers were responding to was obviously a *satisfier*. They totally ignored the elimination of dissatisfiers just as our programmer totally ignored the addition of satisfiers. Shortly thereafter, that programmer left A-Systems, quitting in a fit of frustration. His departure was the beginning of a new culture in our programming department. Since then, every update to our software has intentionally included as many satisfiers as possible and we “brag” about them in each update’s documents. On the other hand, our update documents no longer even mention that bugs were fixed (even though every update will naturally have its share of fixes). Update documents are carefully written to generate “satisfaction” among our users. The result? A-Systems has received fruit baskets, Mardi Gras cakes, pizzas, candy and many other “thank-you’s” from our very *satisfied* clients.

In order to formalize A-Systems’ effort to eliminate all dissatisfiers and maximize the number of satisfiers, we created our own software to track and eliminate all reported “bugs.” The same program has a “Wish List” that tracks every requested “new feature.” To keep our *Wish List* stocked, we actively solicit ideas and then we reward the users who submit the best ideas. To leverage the effect of all the satisfiers we add, we ship multiple updates every year. While, the industry standard is to ship one update per year, we send three. It costs us exactly triple to provide three updates, but it results in a very high level of satisfaction among our software users. At one point, we found that 82% of our new sales came from referrals from existing customers.

Maximizing the number of *satisfiers* in our updates creates very satisfied and very loyal customers!

A note of warning: a satisfier can easily become a dissatisfier. When that former programmer was instructed to add the enhancement I wanted, it was supposed to be added to two places in our software. Doing the minimum amount of work to get by and believing that no one would appreciate the new function anyway, he decided to put it in only one place. When our clients found it in the first place, they were elated. That's when we got the faxes and the positive feedback. When they discovered that the function was not available in the second place—where it should have been, they complained loud and long. This enhancement went from being a satisfier to a dissatisfier in a matter of a couple of days. Needless to say, it was included on the next release. Their response added to the frustration and confusion of the programmer.

When a prospective customer contacts a business, no matter what service or product that business provides, the customer usually has a good idea of *what* the business should be doing for them and *how* the business should be doing it. If we run that business and we disappoint them, they are dissatisfied. Statistically, only a few will complain, but many of them will just go somewhere else, looking for a better place to do business. We will never know why. If we don't disappoint them, it doesn't mean we have successfully created a loyal customer. However, if we do something that goes beyond the normal, we may be providing them with a satisfier. These customers will not only be back, they will refer other customers.

The *key* is to know what our customers perceive as dissatisfiers and satisfiers. If we don't understand the difference, how can we ever give them a "WOW!" experience? Our challenge is to know our customers well enough to quietly eliminate dissatisfiers and then pleasantly surprise them with satisfiers.

At A-Systems, after we started defining our software enhancements based on being either satisfiers or dissatisfiers, an "enlightened" programmer came into my office and proudly announced, "I just added a satisfier." Our present programming team understands the concept and its benefits. It has become an integral part of our corporate culture.

Now, let's extend the concept even further. Satisfiers and dissatisfiers are part of every human relationship. They include employer/employee, husband/wife, parent/child, siblings, friends, and on and on. Knowing what is expected in relationships can reduce disappointments. Adding what is not expected, but will be appreciated, can create the kind of relationships we all want. Understanding the role of satisfiers and dissatisfiers in our lives can change our lives, but only if we make the effort to understand which is which and then *act* on what we know.

In our world, most businesses have an unspoken goal of eliminating dissatisfiers. We make an effort to make it "nice" for our customers. If we go just one step beyond that by adding satisfiers, we will stand out. Our customers will be excited to come back and do business with us. They will be proud to brag about us to their friends.

As an exercise, look around at some of the businesses you deal with and figure out the satisfiers and dissatisfiers in each environment. This simple exercise can effectively open your eyes to opportunities at your own business.

Let's look at some examples. In Salt Lake City, we have several examples that clearly demonstrate the concept. Not far from our former headquarters office was a self-service gas station. People usually go to self service stations for lower price and convenience. It's much faster to pump your own gas and go. Some time ago, the station began to require customers to prepay for the gas they pump. That meant the customer had to enter the building, estimate the amount of their gas purchase, pay for it, return to the car, pump the gas, then retrace their steps into the station to get their change. Only a few blocks away, the competition required only one trip into the building. Which store offered the "convenience" of a convenience store? Prepayment is a dissatisfier.

How about a retail store? Go into most Wal-Marts and you are likely to be greeted by a friendly smile and a warm "Welcome to Wal-Mart." Stores are clean, warm, and friendly. Day after day, week after week, the merchandise is at or near where it was the last time you visited the store. They have removed dissatisfiers and added satisfiers.

Now, return with me to an actual trip I made to a warehouse club, a retail store near our headquarters. This happened in late 2000. The building had been undergoing a minor remodel and construction had dragged on for months, clear into the winter. Winter in Salt Lake City can be severe. (We had the Winter Olympics here in 2002.) Shopping carts were stored outside this warehouse store, literally covered with—you guessed it, snow and ice. They were frozen together, making them nearly impossible to separate. There was a 20-foot wide mud puddle, almost a moat, at the front door. Inside, the store was even less inviting. It was so frigid that you could literally see your breath—inside the store! Customers were expected to shop here? Employees were expected to work here?

Let me describe what I saw one morning as I entered the store. The front of the building was totally torn off. Plastic was covering a gaping hole, a hole that had been there for months. Where were the construction workers? One man was outside drinking coffee and smoking a cigarette. He may have been a contractor or not. There were no others to be found, anywhere. I wandered around the store looking for them. It had been this way for *months*. Store management might blame the builder, but as managers we know that we are responsible for our businesses. Blaming others is a convenience, but it doesn't change reality. In addition to the terrible environment created by extended construction, there were other dissatisfiers.

I had dropped into the store to buy a case of Fritos for our lunchroom. Where were they? During the last three visits, they had been in three places. (Fritos are obviously a favorite of our staff.) I couldn't find them. After about twenty minutes, I gave up. Canned soda pop had been relocated away from where snacks used to be, and *dog food* was now in its place. When I finally found the canned pop, it was located on two aisles. Half was on aisle 17 with cereal. The other half was on aisle 18, next to paper goods. What's wrong with putting it all on aisle 17? That would be convenient, but convenience was not on the minds of the people managing this store! We could go on listing dissatisfiers, but the list was long and incredible. It was a game of "hide and seek" to shop here. If they changed the name of the store to "where? house," it would be more accurate. You actually had to experience it to believe how consistently bad it was. When I went to check out, 4 of the 18 check stands were open. I counted 65 people, cold people, standing in long lines—waiting. I joined them.

There used to be a sign on every register to the effect that "To assure customer satisfaction, any time there are more than three customers in a line, a new register will be opened." That sign may have been conceived by an employee with a cruel sense of humor. I pointed it out the first day it was up—as I stood in a line of *six* customers. The response? They removed the sign! They didn't even pretend to be interested in opening another register. Customer satisfaction was apparently not an issue at this warehouse store, even though we pay an annual fee to shop there.

When I got to the front of the line that wintry day, the cashier asked, "*Did you find everything?*" I said, "*No. How can I if it s in a different place every time I come in?*"

One morning I entered this warehouse store to find the employees standing in the clothing section, while someone dressed in a suit was addressing them. He was explaining that they didn't need to be concerned that the store regularly runs out of items. He explained that the strategy is to artificially stimulate demand for items by running out of them now and then. The strategy is supposed to create an urgency to buy a lot of these "out of stock" items when they *are* available. He assured them that being out of stock was intentional; it was a good thing. I call this the "outhouse strategy," because they are out of stuff so much of the time. I'm a practical shopper. I buy stuff when I need it. If the store doesn't have what I need, I have to go to a store that does. This store's strategy *forced* me to buy a membership at a competing store. I now shop there as often as possible. Their dissatisfiers drove me away.

If we are to succeed at creating customer satisfaction, we need to be aware of these kinds of issues. Customers are not fools and should not be treated as such. We all know good service when we get it. It's a sad statement about our society that we rarely receive it. Even worse, the bad news is that we tolerate it.

The good news is that if our business provides *good* customer service, we stand out as a friendlier, better place for customers to spend their money. Ask yourself these questions: Do I enjoy standing in long lines to purchase goods from a retailer? Why does it take me longer to pay for milk and bread than it does to go to the back of the store, pick them up, and return to the cash registers? Why do I tolerate it? The answer is that we do it because it's always been that way. Bad service may be a tradition, but that doesn't make it right. What traditions can we change in our businesses that will create customer satisfaction? This kind of perspective can change our customer culture.

So, what's the guarantee? If you will identify the satisfiers and dissatisfiers within your business, and make the effort to add satisfiers and eliminate dissatisfiers, you will notice a positive difference in your employees and your customers. As you gain experience in this, your employees will join the effort and your business will stand out compared to the competition. Most businesses treat customers so poorly that you will become a "lighthouse in the night," an orange in a basket of lemons, a diamond in the coal bin. If you doubt that people are treated like cattle, go to the nearest grocery store and see if there are lines of people with carts full of food. Then wander back and forth looking for an open cash register. We are treated like cattle and we accept it.

Let me finish this thought with an example of a great satisfier. I went into *one* of my banks to make a deposit. It was the first of the month. What happens at the first of the month? A lot of retired people go to the bank to cash their social security checks. Sure enough, there were at least 15 people in line. I looked out the window and could see that the drive-ups were filled with cars too. I had no alternative but to wait. I noticed that not every teller window had a teller, but every teller in the branch had her window open. They were doing the best they could. (Unlike my experience with the big warehouse store, waiting in long lines was the exception at this bank, not the rule.) As I waited, I recognized the branch manager when he came into the bank. He was carrying a heavy cooler. He placed it on a table near the line and opened it up.

He introduced himself as the bank manager and apologized that the line was so long. He said it was like "rush hour." Then, he started at the front of the line and asked each customer if they wanted a soda, some orange juice, or a cup of coffee. He personally took care of every single customer! More than half of the people declined his offer, but everyone appreciated the courtesy he demonstrated.

First, this bank manager had eliminated a common bank dissatisfier by having all of the tellers open their windows. That is a novel concept in banking, but he added the satisfier of offering something to drink while we stood in line. I calculated that the whole effort cost the bank less than $20. Unfortunately, few banks would ever consider doing anything like this. The reality here is that decisions at banks are typically made by distant bureaucrats, isolated from actual customers, working at the head office. Real customers are nameless, faceless numbers to them. That's why small banks often provide much better service. We, as small businesses, can do the same thing and we will stand out too. We just need to make it happen.

Here's one final story. A friend purchased a new car, from a local dealership. The salesman followed up with a tin of cookies. It arrived via UPS at his home. It was a nice touch. Six months later, the salesman followed up with a phone call, just checking on how the car was. The result? When my friend knows of anyone looking for a car, he can confidently suggest that they contact his salesman.

Marketing versus Advertising

What is the difference between marketing and advertising, and which one is right for us? These questions must be addressed by every business. It is important to know which will bring the best results for our business. As a general rule, it may be more effective for small businesses to spend money on marketing than on advertising. Of course, advertising may be essential for certain retailers, but we should be skeptical and do everything in our power to control costs. We must spend money where it will do the most good.

When we market, we establish a relationship that drives customers to us in search of our product or service. When we advertise, we compete with every other retailer in the universe trying to get a potential customer's attention, even for a second. Then, we have to convince them that they need our product or service. As I edited this chapter, a magazine publisher sent me a copy of her magazine with a handwritten note, "Let's get you into this issue!" That issue contained 458 pages, with over 1,000 ads! A one-time, 1/3 page ad cost $5,300. Putting the cost aside, what could possibly make a potential customer search us out from among a thousand ads? Just how many ads can a reader see before they blur into one?

Often, our advertising might be compared to "static" on a portable radio, drowned out by the roar of a crowd during the winning touchdown of a football game. Our ads are nothing more than insignificant noise. Advertising is high risk and high cost. We can throw a lot of money away in a big hurry and have nothing to show for it. There are exceptions of course, but be aware of the concept.

So, what is the difference between marketing and advertising? When Exxon created a billboard announcing kerosene for lamps for sale, they were advertising. When they gave away kerosene lamps and sold the kerosene, they were marketing. Once they established a relationship with the customer, the customer became "connected" to Exxon and purchased Exxon kerosene thereafter. This connection went beyond buying goods and services.

Every business needs to get its services and products in front of consumers. If this is not done, we are like the hermit who lives at the edge of town; remember, the one that no one knows about. Advertising is "Hey, look at what I have for you!" Marketing is, "Now that we're friends, have I got a deal for you." It's subtle, but more effective. Because each business is unique, we each have to figure out whether marketing or advertising is better for us. As a small business, we may not have the resources to compete with Wal-Mart® or one of Warren Buffet's mega stores. They spend more on advertising than many retailers gross from sales.

Some of our "traditions" began as marketing strategies. We just don't recognize them for what they are. Describing them might trigger some ideas that will help us see what kind of marketing might help us grow our company.

Every January, a TV network gets us all excited about "THE Super Bowl." Let's cut to the heart of the matter with the precision of a surgeon with a scalpel. The Super Bowl is approximately 16 minutes of actual football action spread over several hours of TV salesmanship. The show attracts millions of viewers who watch the most expensive commercials ever shown on TV. Advertisers spend millions of dollars for the privilege of presenting a few seconds of their story. How is this marketing? The marketing is not done by the advertisers, but by the TV network. They created an audience to sell to advertisers. Feel manipulated? Next

January, decide if you watch the Super Bowl for the football, the advertising, the halftime show, or the hype. If you truly believe you watch the Super Bowl to see football, you are either an incurable armchair quarterback or you are gullible.

Valentine's Day was created to sell cards and gifts. That was marketing genius at work.

A group of fruit growers changed the name of their produce to improve its image. Few knew what a Chinese Gooseberry was. It was brown, furry and ugly. Preppies and yuppies now love their *Kiwi Fruit.* It truly was an effective marketing strategy. Did Shakespeare miss the mark when he condescendingly asked, "What's in a name?"

Restaurant ratings originated in France. A tire company in Paris dominated the market, but car owners were not putting enough miles on their tires. The company published a list of three-star restaurants. (Inflation has driven that up to five-star ratings these days.) Curiously, all of the three-star restaurants were located on the coast, a significant drive from Paris. In order to eat at one of these restaurants you had to use up your tires. Great marketing!

I know a man who wrote a book about how to build your own house, and he marketed his book through seminars. If he were to contact a major national chain of lumber and hardware stores, he would be marketing. That chain could offer his book as a free gift to those individuals who apply for a charge card (a marketing partnership for both a bank and the lumberyard). That's what we mean by marketing. Maybe I should call him and offer that suggestion.

Advertising is not for every product or every business. Have you ever seen an ad for Google? Google is a household name, but they have a reputation for never advertising. Have you ever noticed how much Ralph Lauren advertises on TV? Very little! How about Wal-Mart®? Obviously, they address a totally different customer base.

Have you ever seen a Rolls Royce advertised on TV? How about a Ford? See the difference?

Advertising requires a significant commitment if we are going to accomplish anything. It can't be done on the cheap, with "one-shot, decide now or miss out on my ad campaign" advertising. If we don't do it right, advertising is just background noise, while our deep-pocketed competitors sound like a symphony chorus. For most small businesses, it is safe to suggest that advertising can use up a lot of money in a big hurry. Will it be worth it?

So, what does that leave for a small business? Marketing. What does that mean? It means we have to be creative. That's not a problem, that's the specialty of small business. That's how we have overcome the challenge of having inadequate capital. How can we do this without spending more than the gross national product? Well, we know who our customer is. We know where the customer is. What company can we work with to reach our mutual customers together? What company provides non-competing or complementary products to ours? Is there any way we might form an alliance where we both benefit?

Another option is to create satisfiers that will bond our customers to us. How can we "position" ourselves so customers want to seek us out? We have the right questions. Now we can figure out the answers. In a word, marketing is *out-thinking* our competition. Consider that as a challenge.

Let's face it; marketing is harder than advertising. That's why so few do it. Marketing is better than advertising. That's why those who do it succeed. Successful marketers don't like us to understand their strategy. What they do makes them different. Marketing drives customers to us and, as Peter Drucker said, "...makes selling superfluous." If we are to make the best use of our time and money, we need to consider marketing instead of advertising.

Do you know it all?

Years ago I was hired to manage the financial side of a specialty clinic. My task was to overcome the financial mess created by the clinic's managers (doctors). A salesman stopped by my office one day and wished me good luck with the project. He said, "*Most doctors think MD means Made Deity.* He was being sarcastic, but there was an element of truth to his mockery. Many doctors know so little about business and refuse to admit it, that they are easy marks for the unscrupulous. This particular salesman took a certain pride in outsmarting doctors by taking advantage of their arrogance. He knew that business management and the practice of medicine are separate areas of expertise.

As owners of small business, we often think we must *know* it all because there are so many times when we are required to *do* it all. An entrepreneur must make important decisions about marketing, purchasing, advertising, legal, production, scheduling, finances, hiring and termination, insurance, retirement, and an endless list of other things every day. Often we make these decisions with very limited information and even less insight into what is the ideal thing to do. We often operate our businesses by the seat of our pants! The consequences are often costly, sometimes fatal to a small business.

So, how can we get free advice from wise, experienced people, employees, or outside experts? The first thing to do is call our banker. Specifically, we want to talk to the commercial loan officer, not the one that runs the branch office and approves checks to be cashed, or the one that makes car loans. The one to talk to is the one that makes loans to businesses. They are fountains of knowledge and they cost us nothing.

Like all experts, they can have areas of specialty. Generalists are okay, but if we can find someone who knows our specific industry, we have an ally whose insights are priceless. For instance, there was a banker who had a reputation for being THE banker for the transportation industry. He was my boss, L. Reed Wood. Our branch was located in the suburbs, not in the corner office of the prestigious high-rise in downtown Salt Lake City. Yet, borrowers flocked to our remote location and took their turn, sitting patiently on a cheap couch, waiting for the *opportunity* to discuss their businesses with Reed. His clients were generally quite successful. He was more than a loan officer to them; he was an outside consultant, providing them with free counseling. Over the years, he had learned a lot from dealing with people in the transportation industry (and a lot of other industries) and he shared his valuable insights and suggestions with his list of lucky clients.

During this time, a large transportation company in Salt Lake City was acquired by a new owner. He was from out of state. He approached our bank for financing, but he preferred to do *his* banking downtown, where he could rub shoulders with the senior executives of the bank. It was probably a status thing. Unfortunately, they did not have the same level of expertise as Reed. While the competition continued to prosper, the new owner of that trucking company got himself into financial difficulties that would lead to bankruptcy. By the time Reed was asked to be involved, it was too late. Could that business owner have done better if he had sought out a banker with expertise in his industry? Would he have been wise to ask around, seeking a banker that understood his business better? We suspect so. Is there a lesson for us?

What about insurance? Can we know it all? Top insurance sales people have years of specialized training and experience. They do not charge anything for answering questions. They make money when we buy their products. They have solutions to problems we never knew existed. Is it worth a call? What if we develop a relationship where we can trust an insurance expert to recommend the best product, not just the one that gives them the highest commission?

What about legal expertise? Can we afford to save money on an attorney? Would we ask our family doctor to do a heart transplant? Lawyers have areas of expertise just like doctors. Are we best served by experts? Will we pay more? Will it be worth it?

What about management consulting firms? Are they good? It depends. Are they experts in our industry or are they experts in marketing their services? Several times a year I get calls from firms that want to come in and tell me how to run my business. They insist that they are experts. They claim they know more than I do about my business because they are experts "generally." They get their feet in the door and before unsuspecting entrepreneurs know it, these "experts" have racked up $30,000 in bills.

The owner of one small business actually paid them $30,000 for their "expertise"—then he filed for bankruptcy. The consulting firm knew very little about his business, especially compared to the insights of the owner. After they left, he said he should have charged them for his time.

While I am a bit disparaging toward consultants generally, I admit that I have worked as one. When I took an assignment, it took time to learn the unique characteristics of the industry, the individual business, its competition, its management, their strategies, their products and services, and their market presence before I could offer a meaningful contribution. And, this time was all paid for by the client.

Was I worth it? I provided a fresh, outside perspective on an old situation, something existing management could not do.

Let me provide an example. Once upon a time I worked for a small company that was acquired by a huge public company. The high-priced MBAs from the new parent company were charged with improving profitability. Unfortunately, they missed out on a fact of life not typically discussed in MBA schools, something known as "the good ol' boy network." Without revealing the identities of the guilty, the MBA "gunslingers" were determined to justify their big salaries by cutting costs in our subsidiary. One of our highest-profile costs was our trading group, members of the invisible good ol' boy network, which generated millions of dollars in high-margin transactions every month. The MBAs replaced our extremely well paid, demanding, and finicky members of the good ol' boy network with low paid, rank amateurs who could be told what to do and how to do it. In no time, the good ol' boy network began to chew up our novices and spit them out. Thus began an immediate decline in high-margin transactions. The slide continued until our company was losing money every month. In short order, the MBAs (derisively called "hatchet men") caused the failure of the business they were supposed to be improving. Perhaps an outsider with nothing to prove would not have ruined a successful company. Perhaps independence is an asset. This case might be an exception, so my skepticism stands. Be careful about engaging outside consultants.

Let me offer an example of a valuable consultant. He only worked in one industry. He knew the industry far better than most of his clients. He could spot problems and lay out solutions before his technically expert clientele understood what he was doing or how he was doing it. He dazzled management with his operational insights. He was good. In the 1980's, he charged $1,000 per day plus expenses. He was worth every penny. Today, he could charge a multiple of that and still be “cheap.” There aren’t many like him.

The *process* he used was his strength. It was simple and it could be used by almost anyone to get good results. He interviewed every employee twice. In the first round of interviews, he asked them to define the problems in the operation, whether it was in their area or not. Sometimes it was personnel, sometimes it was a process or a procedure, but there was always a long list of things that could be improved.

In the second round of interviews, he asked each employee to define the solutions to the problems uncovered during the initial interviews. The results were amazing. Let’s face some basic truths. The world’s greatest experts on unloading trucks are found on the loading dock. The people that face this task everyday know there are better ways. The problem is that no one ever asks them for their opinion. As a result, they feel no one cares about improving things. No one appreciates what these *experts* could do for the business, so they keep their ideas to themselves.

If we can get our employees involved, they will gladly contribute valuable insights that can make our business succeed. The cost is far less than any consultant, and the benefits include more than money—morale is improved too.

Why would we want to do this ourselves? It will generate information we need, virtually for free. It will uncover problems that we may not even know about. It has the potential to generate solutions we would never think of. So, what is the risk? What if *we* are the biggest problem within our business? What if we happen to be the factor that will be the cause of our business’s failure? What if we are such jerks that we are oblivious to this fact? This is often the case, but our employees aren’t going to tell us. This might be when an outside consultant might be the only way to get to the bottom of the problem, but be careful. The sad truth is that some "consultants" have such weak spines they only tell their clients what they want to hear. These consultants waste our time and money.

Some years ago, I was an employee of a company that hired a "Big 6" accounting firm. They had just finished their audit work and were compiling their findings so they could make recommendations to the parent company. In jest, I quietly asked the lead auditor if he wanted "to know where the bodies are buried?" I was just curious to know if he was interested in knowing if management had successfully deceived him and his staff by hiding facts that could materially impact his report on the company. He declined my offer coldly and immediately exited my office. Apparently, he wanted to get his fee paid and go on. I'm not sure how I would have responded if he had wanted the information I was offering. I was totally surprised when he turned his back on my offer, whether it was real or in jest.

Sometimes, outsiders are only interested in telling us what we want to hear and getting paid for it. That's not good enough. In small business, the best results often come when we do it ourselves. First, we usually can't afford outsiders. Second, we hope we understand every facet of our business.

Finally, there are a number of resources we can rely on to provide expert assistance for free or at nominal cost. First on that list is the U.S. Small Business Administration (the SBA). Within the SBA is SCORE, the Service Core of Retired Executives. These guys can be wonderful. Often, they are successful entrepreneurs whose businesses were bought out or they are retired experts. Many of them are fountains of knowledge and wisdom. In my experience with SCORE, I found that their offices are either very good or just the opposite. The force that drives them, the thing that determines whether they are useful or just an entrepreneur's social club is generated internally, on a local basis, not provided by Washington, D.C.

Many universities and colleges have Small Business Development Centers (SBDCs). Both students and professional consultants are there to work with local businesses. They can be an affordable source of useful help. As with SCORE, each SBDC has its own personality, value, and level of expertise.

Procurement Technical Assistance Centers (PTACs) are there to help small businesses secure government contracts. Many PTACs are go-getters, but a number of them are staffed only with bureaucrats. Many Chambers of Commerce have assistance and referral services too. Most states and many cities have economic development offices that provide different types of assistance to small businesses, most at minimal or no cost.

As business owners, we simply cannot know it all, but we can get expert advice without spending huge sums for outside consultants. If we want to do it ourselves and if we are willing to invest the time, we can literally duplicate the process used by successful consultants and save a fortune.

Can you do it all?

As a matter of survival, we often find ourselves *trying* to do it all. Part of this is due to limited resources, part of it is expediency, and part may be a matter of overconfidence.

In the last chapter, the methods used by an outside consultant were described in enough detail that any business manager could use them. This was included to encourage us to do those things that we can do for ourselves. This chapter offers what may be viewed as a conflicting suggestion. It is the reality that we simply cannot do it all ourselves and do it well, so there are some things we may better off having someone else do. We have to evaluate things as we go.

There is nothing wrong with doing all we can. Certainly, we are better managers when we know everything we can about our business, the products and services we use, and the products and services we provide. When we have personally performed the tasks our employees are expected to do, we have powerful insights into what it takes to run our businesses. When an employee is wasting time or doing something inappropriate, our personal experience assures that we will easily recognize what is going on. Unfortunately, this kind of control and insight may only exist in an *ideal* world.

Back to the real world (the world where we must make real money) we simply cannot *do it all.* There are not enough hours in the day and we don't *know it all.* Often, we are better off if we use outside experts for certain products and services. This is often referred to as outsourcing. Contractors do it all the time. They call it "subcontracting." Outsourcing can save our business, even build it to unforeseen levels. There is value in specializing in what we do well and using other's expertise to take us to heights we could not reach ourselves.

Let's consider a story that demonstrates this concept. It will help us see the need for a strategy: be all that we can be by focusing on our area of expertise. Doing that, we can maximize our output, our efficiency, and, best of all, our profitability.

Imagine for a minute that there are only two businesses in our town. They are owned by Bill and Sally. Bill lives on the hill, Sally in the valley. Bill and Sally each have 200 acres. Both try to "do it all" themselves and they do a pretty good job. Let's consider what would happen if they specialized at what they do best and outsourced their other needs to each other? Could they do better, make more money? Would our whole town be better off?

The soil on the hill where Bill lives is rocky and uneven. The temperature is cool. It is not good soil for farming, but it is great for raising sheep and wool. Because Bill insists on doing it all, he raises sheep on half of his two hundred acres and he does his best to grow wheat on the other half. He gets 6 hundred-pound bundles of wool per acre, but only 35 bushels of wheat per acre. Bill has a competitive advantage when raising sheep.

Sally has a farm in the valley. Sally has great soil, warm and fertile, perfect for farming, but not as good for raising sheep and wool. Sally insists on doing it all too, so she grows wheat on half of her two hundred acres and she tries to raise sheep on the other half. She gets 70 bushels of wheat per acre, but only 3 hundred-pound bundles of wool per acre. Here is the gross product of our town:

	Wool	Wheat
Bill's Production	600 bundles	3,500 bushels
Sally's Production	+300 bundles	+7,000 bushels
Total Production	900 bundles	10,500 bushels

What would happen if Bill raised only sheep, Sally raised only wheat, and they traded half their annual harvest to each other? Would either of them be better off? Might our whole country be better off, with a greater GNP?

If Bill raised only sheep, he could produce 1,200 bundles of wool per year (6 per acre x 200 acres). If Sally raised only wheat, she could produce 14,000 bushels per year (70 bushels per acre x 200 acres).

	Wool	Wheat
Bill's Total Production	1,200 bundles	
Sally's Total Production		14,000 bushels
Bill's New Half	600 bundles	7,000 bushels
Bill Old Half	-600 bundles	-3,500 bushels
Bill's Gain	0	3,500 bushels
Sally's New Half	600 bundles	7,000 bushels
Sally Old Half	-300 bundles	-7,000 bushels
Sally's Gain	300 bundles	0

If they traded exactly half of their harvest to each other, they would both be ahead! Bill would have 3,500 extra bushels of wheat and Sally would have 300 additional bundles of wool. The town's total productivity was increased by 33%. The whole town is wealthier because they specialized in doing what they did well. Economists have an impressive technical term for this, something like "maximizing economic efficiency." We call it "doing what you do best."

Efficiency can be much more than maximizing production. In small business, we need to keep our eyes open for opportunities where our expertise, our service, or our product can be bundled with someone else's expertise, service, or product; where the combination will result in something like 2 + 2 = 5 or 6 or even more.

Years ago I was writing credit reports in downtown Salt Lake City. After I finished writing a report for Lorry's Shirt Shop, I discovered that a second business was located at the same address. Lorry told me that the owner of that business had started a shirt business. He was creating a new brand. He had shirts manufactured out of the country to very strict quality specifications. His shirts were shipped to Salt Lake City where a bunch of Mormon ladies, who were handy with sewing machines, embroidered his unique "logo." (The most fashionable logo at that time was supposed to be an alligator, but after the shirt was washed the first time, the alligator looked more like a dead bug stuck to your shirt.)

After this guy's shirts got their hand-embroidered logo, they were shipped to the garment district in New York City for distribution. Lorry said that I was just lucky because the owner just happened to be there that day. Usually he was in New York City or some other part of the world. Lorry pointed to what looked like a closet door, located on the west side of his store. Behind it was a steep, narrow staircase, going up to the second floor. The white paint on the steps was cracked and peeling. As I walked up the stairs, they creaked noisily. Light came from a painted-over window, situated about half way up and to the right of the stairs.

As I got to the window, I met someone coming down. The man asked if he could help me. Obviously, there was not a lot of traffic on these stairs, so he guessed I was there on business. I handed him my business card, introduced myself, and said I was there to write a credit report. I told him that I was looking for Ralph Lauren. He said, "*I m Ralph Lauren.*" We compiled his credit report and I left, not knowing the "celebrity" of the man I had just interviewed. The next time I saw Ralph Lauren's face it was on the cover of *Time Magazine*, where he was called the "$600 Million Man."

The reason for this story is not to be a name-dropper. (Well, maybe just a little. How many of *you* have met Ralph Lauren?) The point is that Ralph Lauren doesn't personally make the house paint, perfume, eyeglass frames, bed sheets, hats, shoes, volleyballs, furniture, etc. that bear his name. Ralph Lauren's specialty is maintaining a prestigious image that sells for a premium through distribution channels that serve people wanting the best product on the market. He only teams up with people who meet his high standards for quality, but don't have either the name recognition or the international distribution channel he does. The combination benefits both parties. He makes easy money on other people's products and they sell a lot more product, at a profit, because of their alliance with Ralph Lauren.

In fact, Ralph Lauren's image has become so elite that people have taken to pronouncing his name as "Ralflo-wren" instead of "Ralf Lore-un", adding something exotic. In truth, his name is Ralph Lifschitz, the son of Frank and Frieda Lifschitz, Russian immigrants. Is that marketing or what?

If we were in the business of manufacturing and we were approached by the "Ralph Lauren" of our industry, would we be willing to "private label" our product in order to sell more of it? What if we were able to sell ten times as much, a hundred times, a thousand times? Sounds like an easy decision to me. For Ralph Lauren, this is outsourcing at its ultimate. For his vendors, they get to use someone else's image and distribution channel. Both do what they do best!

All businesses do outsourcing of one kind or another all the time. For instance, who printed our last full color brochure or sales sheet? Did we spend seven figures for a top-of-the-line Heidelberg press or did we call a printer to do it for us? Who delivered our last overnight package across the country? Did we have one of our employees hand deliver it for us or did we call FedEx and have them pick it up at our door and deliver it to our customer's door? Obviously, there are very good reasons to use experts to complement our operating skills.

At A-Systems, we use outsourcing just like everyone else. We develop accounting software for small business. When A-Systems has large runs of CDs, we can contract with a company here in Salt Lake City to do the duplication. Of course we have duplicating machines for smaller runs, but when the need is for thousands of CDs in a hurry, it's far more convenient, much faster, and only marginally more costly to have an outsider do it. We don't have to invest in the kind of equipment necessary to produce a thousand CDs per hour or hire the staff, which would only be busy now and then. In the long run, it actually costs us less.

We now have two perspectives to the question on the table. If we focus on doing what we do best, what is there in our business that might be outsourced to reduce our costs? Two, who can we form an alliance with to market our products and services, thereby increasing our sales?

Some of A-Systems' construction clientele refer to themselves as construction managers. In theory, they "build" shopping malls, high-rises, or residential developments. They generate revenue in the millions of dollars per month, yet they have only a handful of actual employees. How do they do this? They use subcontractors to do the actual work. One company builds and operates shopping malls in southern California. Besides the owner, there are only two employees. Everything else is subcontracted. Their highly profitable operation is based on their expertise of developing and managing malls. All of the actual physical construction is handled by outside experts. They deal with a long list of subcontractors, from surveyors to landscapers, from roofers to plumbers, as they "build" a shopping mall. In the end, they do not drive a single nail. This is outsourcing at its finest.

In the fall of 1972, I met with the owner of a unique business. He was in the "motel" business. His "chain" was headquartered in a small office in his home. Hundreds of motels joined his chain to get the benefits of "pooled purchasing" of supplies. Purchases were made through the chain and "drop shipped" directly to members. In fact, the owner was the only employee. Eventually, he merged into another chain and he retired a very wealthy man. Members of his chain "outsourced" purchasing through him and benefited with lower costs. Remember, every dollar saved by reducing costs goes to the bottom line.

Your Dreams

Most people are reluctant to openly discuss their dreams. We keep dreams private because no one wants to be mocked when things don't go the way we hoped. We have to get over that. In the real world, things *never* go according to plan. That's reality. Adjustments need to be made regularly. Timing is changed, strategies are amended, and resources are reallocated all the time. That's real life and that's why a computer can't run a business. It takes the vision, judgment, and leadership of an entrepreneur.

So, if nothing goes as planned, what good are dreams? Dreams are the long-range goals we reach for. If we have no vision of what we want the future to hold, how can we ever achieve it? Success rarely happens by accident. *We* have to know what we want and *we* have to make it happen. Let's consider the conversation that Alice had with the Cheshire Cat in *Alice in Wonderland*.

> Alice asked, "Would you tell me, please, which way I ought to go from here?"
>
> "That depends a good deal on where you want to get to," said the Cat.
>
> "I don't much care where..." said Alice.
>
> "Then it doesn't matter which way you go," interrupted the Cat.
>
> "...so long as I get somewhere," Alice added as an explanation.
>
> "Oh, you're sure to do that," said the Cat, "if you only walk long enough."

Like Alice, if we don't know *where* we want to go, how can we possibly figure out *how* to get there? What's more, if we actually do manage to get somewhere, how will we know when we have arrived?

We are going to do an exercise that will help you envision where you want to go and then outline what it will take to get there. For some, envisioning the future can be difficult. If we accept the conclusions of Dr. Roger Sperry (1913-1994), who worked with people with brain damage, the left side of the brain controls different functions than the right side of the brain. Some consider his work controversial, but it certainly explains why some of us are artistic, but can't balance a checkbook, while others can unravel a geometry theorem, but can't make their clothes match.

So, here is Sperry's theory: Our left-brain "thinks." This is where our logical, analytical functions are housed. Our right-brain "feels." This is where our creativity and aesthetics are housed. Have you ever wondered why conservatives and liberals never see eye to eye? Different sides of their brains are dominant. They think differently, so they define their experiences from totally different perspectives. I heard someone ask, "Why are there so many liberals in the entertainment industry?" Entertainers, artists, etc. tend to be right-brained. Consider Robin Williams and Julia Roberts, talented actors, who are very liberal-minded. It's their strength *and* their weakness. Someone else asked, "Why do technical people seem so detached emotionally." It's their strength *and* their weakness. Some people may have more balanced brains, but most of us are stronger in one area than the other.

So, what does this mean to us as entrepreneurs? Some of us naturally think more logically than others. Others of us are born to be more visionary or with more creative "juices" than others. This is something of a paradox. Those who think more logically tend to be less visionary and those who are visionary tend to be poor at implementing their vision. To truly succeed in business, we need both.

Let's prepare to participate in an exercise that requires both logic *and* vision. Rather than allow anyone to fail because of a strong left-brain, I'm going to guide you through it, one step at a time. Once you learn the process, you can repeat this exercise as often as necessary. As we progress, your mind will probably start churning out a rapid succession of thoughts and ideas. Write them down and don't talk about them until *after* you have written them down. Talking uses a different part of the left-brain, interrupting the process we are stimulating.

We're going to use your right-brain to take a little journey in time. You are going on a trip into the future to tour your business when it is everything you want it to become. You are going to visualize your success. Let's start.

First, have a pad and a pen within reach. Sit in a comfortable chair, possibly at a desk or table, where you won't be disturbed for at least an hour. (That can be a challenge for an entrepreneur.) If you have anything in your hands, put it down, shake your hands out, and let them relax. Lean back and get comfortable in your chair. Take a deep breath, let it out, and do it again. We want your senses and attention to be focused on your mind's experiences. You will want to close your eyes after you understand the instructions. If you prefer, have someone read the instructions while you listen, with your eyes closed. After they read the instructions, they should leave you alone in the room.

We are taking a journey into the future about five years from now. We are going to the time when you are successful, a time when you have finally "arrived." As we begin, you are driving down the street in a new car. You can smell the "newness" of it. The leather seats squeak when you move. The steering is tight and responsive. The ride is smooth. Music from your Bose® stereo fills your ears. As you arrive at the front of your business, turn in and stop for a second. What do you see? First, what kind of building is it? Is it brick, block, or wood frame? What does the sign look like? Is it white with black letters or have you chosen something more colorful, with neon? Your building tells everyone you are successful. There is a parking lot with the trucks and equipment used in your business. There is plenty of room for customer parking. Your parking lot has a fresh seal on it and newly repainted white stripes contrast against the back asphalt. What else do you see as you look around? Take it all in. Look at the details that speak of your success.

Now, walk inside your building. What do you see when you enter? Look at the framed pictures of satisfied customers on the wall. They impress prospective customers. They impress you too. Now, cross the main area or room and go down the hall to your private office. What does your office look like? Notice that even the carpet speaks of your success. Do you have a desk? Or, is it more of a worktable? What kind of chair is behind your desk? Is it leather or fabric? Is there a computer on your desk? What kind of phone do you have? Notice that the phone lines are lit up with customers! The place radiates success! On the wall there are a number of plaques and awards you've received, accolades from your industry. There are framed newspaper articles written about your business hanging on the wall. You are well known and respected; you have a good image.

Now, let's move into another room, maybe a conference room, where your employees are waiting, ready for you to give a little speech. You can smell the coffee. Everyone is talking and smiling. It's noisy. The room is filled with good people. They enjoy working here. Today they are waiting for you to inspire them so they can fulfill your vision of success. You feel well prepared for today's meeting. It gives you a good feeling to be here. Look around. How many employees are there? Do you recognize your best employees as you scan the room? How many teams or crews do you have? What a great bunch of people you have assembled! They have done a lot to earn your respect and the respect of your customers. They look to you to lead them, so they will know what needs to be done. With that trust and respect, they work hard and you reward them well. You respect and value your employees because they are an important part of your success.

Now, consider your customers and look at your business through their eyes. You have an enviable reputation. You are admired. Your company is respected. What is there about you and your company that justifies such a positive reputation? What kind of image have you created? Certainly, your hard work and integrity have paid off handsomely, but there is something else that makes you different. What is it? Ponder this for a minute: What makes you so unique? How do you differentiate your business from your competition? This is a very important concept. You may want to revisit this question over and over as you think back about this process.

Now, envision everything you want in order to consider your business a *success*. Study every detail. This vision of your future, your definition of success, is what you want to bring into reality. After you have become familiar enough with this vision that you can describe it in detail, the next step begins.

Now, you need to look back at what you started doing five years ago to get where you are today. The left side of your brain has to do its part now. Specifically, what *changes* did you make five years ago that resulted in what you have become? These will be your "projects." Be logical, sequential, and detail minded. These *projects* are what you had to do to get where you are and they are very important.

Here are some more questions you may want to ponder as you unfold your vision of the future. What qualities or values did you instill into your employees that created your reputation? How and where did you find such a great bunch of employees? What training did they receive? What vision did you give them to make them so dedicated? What marketing strategies did you use to expand your business so smoothly? What relationships or alliances did you make that bring you to the attention of so many customers? Exactly how do your customers find you? What is there about your product and your service that keeps your customers coming back? And finally, why do they refer their friends? These questions are designed to assist you in the analysis of your vision.

Now, let's get personal. What is there about your personality that makes you a successful leader? You need to exploit your strengths as much as possible. What about the other side? Which of your personality traits (or quirks) did you have to overcome to succeed? This is important. None of us are perfect. We need to recognize our personal weaknesses in order to compensate for them. This is a very private part of your business plan, but it cannot be ignored. Be realistic.

After you have completed your tour of the future, take the next hour (or whatever time it takes) and write down your thoughts. Don't talk to anyone about what you saw yet. You are in a state of heightened awareness, so immediately write *what you saw* in very specific detail. This is your *definition of success*.

The next step is to write down all of the projects that were required to bring your vision to reality. (This is where the left side of your brain goes to work.) This may be the most important thing you will ever do as an entrepreneur. You are outlining a plan to bring your "vision" into reality. Some have reported that this part of the exercise gave them incredible insights. One entrepreneur confessed, "I knew exactly what I wanted to become, but it wasn't until I used this technique that I realized I wasn't *doing* a single thing to make it happen. Wow!"

The final step is a charting process. Here is where you prioritize all of the projects that need to be done. Which project must be accomplished first? Which project requires another project to be finished first? Which may happen simultaneously? How long will each take? Now, create a timeline listing each project, in its sequential order. Calculate a beginning date for each one. Show an ending date and then add the projects that will follow this one. Finally, list each of these projects on a spreadsheet, starting with the first project on the left side, sequentially adding subsequent projects to the right. After they are all listed with start and end dates, connect the project with lines, creating a flow chart. What you have just charted is known as the "critical path" to your future.

Remember something. Your *critical path* is written on paper (or an electronic spreadsheet), *not* in concrete. It can change. In fact, you must *plan* for change. Some projects will develop faster than you expect. A few may even happen by themselves. You must be prepared to move forward. Some steps within a project may take much longer than you want. You must be patient and not give up. You may need to change tactics. A few things may not happen at all. Compensate. That's life.

What you have just created is a big part of a *Business Plan*. Combine this information with your SWOT Analysis and your Cash Forecasts and you should have most of the essential information needed in a good Business Plan. But what you have in front of you is more than just a plan; it is your *vision.* Your plan is simply a tool to bring your vision into reality. When your employees know and understand your vision, they can do their part to implement the plan too.

There is a story about a good man who wanted to do good things for needy people. He had a generous heart and a strong faith in God. He prayed for months to win the lottery so he could use the money to help other people. On the day of the drawing, he did not win. For the next lottery, he fasted and prayed. He gave up certain things he considered to be sins so he could be worthy of winning. Again, on the day of the drawing he did not win. Crushed, he knelt in prayer asking God for an explanation. After all, he was a good man with a good heart, he had fasted and prayed, he had worked hard to become worthy, and he wanted to do a good thing. As he finished his prayer, a quiet voice whispered to his heart, "*Buy a ticket.*"

All the good intentions and desire in history will not do a bit of good if we don't do the right things to bring them into reality. This man did things right, but he didn't do the right things.

One last word of warning: be sure to keep your focus. Sometimes it's hard to remember that your goal was to drain the swamp, when you're up to your neck in alligators. Always remember what you are trying to accomplish.

Let me suggest a competitive strategy: Play *your* game by *your* rules, not *their* game by *their* rules. Let me explain that with an example. A-Systems is an accounting software company. A-Systems will never be able to outspend our competitors, Microsoft and Intuit, playing *their* game by *their* rules. We had to envision a way to compete with them where we could win. First, our products had to be designed to be superior to theirs. We used a variety of strategies to make our software "quick to learn and easy to use." Second, our service had to be superior too. Third, we had to charge less because our customers are small businesses, people with limited budgets. Delivering superior products and services at a lesser price was an ambitious vision, but it was *our* game. At A-Systems, we aren't going to sell software to everyone, just the ones who want better software for less and the ones who like old-fashioned personal service. When someone looks at our software and says, "*Your software (or your company) is certainly different from Intuit (or Microsoft),*" we respond, "*Thank you!*"

We set our own standards and made our own rules. From the start, we kept our eyes on our long-term goals as we built our product line and our company. We could not cut corners and maintain the quality of our software and the integrity of our service. The same goes for your business. We believe that small businesses can thrive in markets dominated by huge companies. The *size* of big business is their greatest weakness. They can never respond to customers and develop personal relationships the way small businesses can. That is *the* vulnerability entrepreneurs have to exploit. Let's face it, in business it's the big guys against the little guys, us against them. That's reality. If A-Systems can successfully compete with huge companies, perhaps your business can do the same thing. You just have to make new rules to play by.

One more insight, big business is forced to protect the status quo because they are so heavily invested in it. Small business can move ahead quickly and evolve by bringing superior products and services to the market. For instance at A-Systems, we ship three updates per year, not the traditional *annual* update released by the big guys. Our aggressive delivery of new conveniences and timesaving functions is deeply appreciated by the people who use our software. What about bug fixes? If a bug is found, we quickly fix it and put it on our website so it can be downloaded—for free. We have a little program built into our software that automatically checks our website to see if there are any updates to be downloaded. Our clientele can download them any time they want.

On top of that, we go one step further. We keep our focus by providing the kind of old-fashioned personal customer service that neither Microsoft nor Intuit can compete with. Live bodies answer our phones, not machines. There is no maze of recorded menus to work your way through. Those answering our phones are in the US, not India or some other offshore facility. When a question is asked, we have an answer, unique to that customer. Our technical people don't look at a screen to read an answer from a scripted computer program. In addition to providing quality products and services, we provide jobs to the US economy, just like your business.

In order for A-Systems to compete in the software industry, it was necessary for us to discover our strengths, develop them, and build *our* rules around them. The same strategy might work for you. What is there about your business, your product, or service that you can focus on? What is contained in the vision of your success that you can develop as a "theme," to keep in your mind at all times? Remember the suggestion to find something that differentiates your business from the competition? This is where you use it. This is one of the right things to do.

The Trap

Many owners of small businesses fall into "the trap." They do not understand something we have repeated over and over. There is a difference between *doing things right* and *doing the right things*! Technical types typically do things right. Wise entrepreneurs do the right things. If this doesn't mean anything to you, go back to the chapter on *Dreams*. You need a vision that you can work to fulfill. With that vision, you will understand what the *right things* are.

The French word, "entrepreneur" literally means "undertaker." It does not mean the best cabinetmaker, the most skilled electrician, the most creative copywriter, or any title that applies to a technical or creative skill. Success in operating a business has very little to do with being a technical expert. What? "This is an insult to experts!" someone suggests. It's time to get real. The unfortunate truth is that many technical experts go into business without the business skills necessary to survive the first payroll. As a result, many, if not most, technical types fail. When technical types focus on doing things right, they *assume* they are doing the right things. They work *in* the business not *on* the business. Sadly, in many cases, they are doing little more than "straightening deck chairs on the Titanic."

The PC was invented in Salt Lake City. The creator, clearly a visionary genius, was left with nothing to show for his innovation. His business failed. In fact, he admitted that he failed at several businesses. Did he do things right or did he do the right things? Ask him and he would never acknowledge there was a difference. That's why he failed.

As creative and intelligent as he was and as hard as he worked, he died in *poverty.*

While interviewing business owners at Dun & Bradstreet, I observed certain patterns. One obvious pattern was what happened to a business when an attorney got control. With a few notable exceptions, they promptly went out of business for one reason or other. Technical skills do not guarantee the presence of entrepreneurial expertise. Attorneys are a perfect example of technical experts who know how to do things right, but don't necessarily know the right things to do. With all due respect for their years of education and hard work, some doctors and attorneys suffer from intellectual arrogance. As a result, they cannot accept that they do not know how to run a business.

When we focus exclusively on doing things right and hope everything else will somehow magically fall into place, it's like that jet mentioned earlier that lost its gyroscopic compass. The captain announced, "*We don t know where we re going, but we re certainly making good time.*"

The responsibilities inherent in running a small business are very diverse. We may find ourselves negotiating an important sale one morning and buying office supplies that afternoon. We wear a lot of hats. We are the ones that have to *do* what must be done. We must be careful in all of our *doing* that we do not forget that one of our most important hats, the hat of leader, cannot gather dust. We must always remember to be working *on* the business while we work *in* it.

Management versus Leadership

Running a small business is not a "passive" activity. It requires us to be visionary *and* to lead by high-profile example. It often requires us to know what needs to be done *and* how to do it. Leaders have the ultimate responsibility for determining which are the right things to do. Effective leaders *delegate* the details to technical types, who are responsible to do things right. Leaders envision the future *and* define the steps necessary to get there, as outlined in the chapter on *Dreams*.

As the owners of small businesses, we need to be both leaders *and* managers, filling *both* roles if we are to achieve success. In small business, neither role will succeed without the other. The other reality is that wearing so many hats can create serious conflicts in our thought processes. With each change of hat, we must remember to change our mindset, to think and act differently in each responsibility. It is very much like being an actor playing multiple roles. If this is unclear, go back to the chapter on *Dreams*.

Thousands of books have been written on all aspects of this thing we call leadership (just as with every other subject we've covered). We have focused only on that one characteristic which is most relevant to succeeding in small business: doing the right things. It is up to us to set the course for our businesses by making sure the right things are being done to get us there. That is leadership. That is our challenge.

Small Business and the Economy

In 1988, the results of an 18-year long survey were reported in the *Wall Street Journal.* What was revealed was counter to the accepted way of thinking. During that period, Fortune 500 companies (big business) had actually eliminated jobs while the rest of the economy got credit for creating new jobs. For every two jobs eliminated by Fortune 500 companies, eleven new jobs were created by non Fortune 500 companies. This statistic was a slap in the face to entrenched, old-line economists who continually preached to the highest levels of US government that the health of our economy depended on what happens in big business.

The results of the survey came as no surprise to those of us in small business or anyone else in touch with the economic events reported in newspapers or on the evening news. Since the 1970s, big business has become synonymous with "down-sizing." Defenders of the faith have tried to *spin* that as "right-sizing" while cynics label it "dumb-sizing." Whatever the name, the reality is the same. Big business destroys jobs, while small business creates jobs. It is this reality that assures us *our* contribution is meaningful and positive. We are *very* important to the US economy.

It may not be "politically correct" to brag about this, but the economy of the world is interwoven with and highly dependent upon what happens in the US economy. The dastardly events of September 11th bruised the native self-confidence we feel as Americans. As a consequence, we quickly "fell" into a recession, something the economy had been slowly sliding toward during the reign of Clinton and Gore. Our recession rippled across the globe.

Now let's pull all of this together into a surprising conclusion. The US economy is the most powerful force in the economic world, but we know the US economy relies on small business for its vitality. Therefore, the world economy is directly dependent on or highly influenced by what happens in US small business! That's us, you and me.

Why is this? The first thing is job creation, as was demonstrated by the study. The second is innovation and creativity. Was the PC invented by the largest computer company in the world or by a dinky little company in Utah named Sphere Corporation? Was the most powerful program of all time, the electronic spreadsheet, created by a big company or two guys calling themselves Personal Software? Did IBM create the operating system used on the PC or was it a guy who worked at a computer shop in Tukwila, Washington? The examples go on and on and on and on.

We conclude logically that the most significant *positive* economic force in the world is *small business.* The economic success of the world is in many ways dependent upon what happens in small business everywhere, in every country. It's not big business. It's not government. It's *especially* not government. Contrary to what politicians might espouse, government is not a *positive* economic force, but we know that small business is exactly that. And, we know that the secret to *our* success is doing the right things.

The Meaning of Life in Business

You have now completed the requirements for your MBA. At commencement exercises, we traditionally hear uplifting and motivational speeches, designed to challenge us and inspire us to make the effort necessary to succeed. Every graduate deserves a commencement speech, so here is yours.

On Sundays, I have the opportunity to teach about the meaning of life. The questions most often asked are:

- Who am I?
- Where did I come from?
- Why am I here?
- Where am I going?

Let's put the welfare of our souls aside and ask these questions from our perspective as the owners of small businesses. Those who understand the answers to these questions do far better in business, and in life, for that matter. With that thought, the following insights are offered for your contemplation.

Who am I? You are an entrepreneur. *You* are the one behind the business. It is *not* the technology or the collective technical skills of your employees. It is *not* your product. It is *not* your service. It is *you*. As the entrepreneur, *you* are the "glue" that holds everything together, the visionary that empowers the business and your employees. Your success is up to you.

Where did I come from? You came from a unique background. Your *education* is unique. From elementary school through college, what you learned from each class, from each teacher, and from each textbook is unique to you. You did not receive the same things from your education that anyone else did, even if someone actually sat next to you in all of your classes, was taught by the same teachers, and used the same textbooks. You obtained what was uniquely important to you. You learned what you wanted to know.

Your *skills* are unique to you. What you know how to do is a reflection of your personal drive and self discipline. The skills you chose to acquire and how much time you put into learning them is totally unique to you. No one has the same set of skills you do.

Your *talents* are unique to you too. No one was born with the same abilities and strengths you have. While we celebrate the proposition that all men are created equal, the concept may apply to our rights, but it certainly has nothing to do with the talents we were born with. Some of us have a "tin" ear. Others can sing like a songbird. Some of us run like walruses. Others are as graceful as gazelles. Some of us fear heights. Others love to climb the faces of cliffs with no safety equipment. What is inborn in each of us is clearly unique. We are *not* born equal; we were born unique.

Your *ambitions* are unique to you. What you want to accomplish, what you want to become, and how you want to be remembered are each unique to you. Your dreams are unique.

Your *heritage* is unique to you also. Aside from your DNA, your legacy as a member of a family is unique to you. The values your parents taught you, the relationships you established with each member of your family and your friends, the way you learned to interact with others, and the value you place on other people combine to make you unique.

Put all of these unique facets together and you have a combination that no one else, anywhere in the world, at any time in history has ever had. You are, without a doubt, totally unique.

Why am I here? You are here to contribute something meaningful to the world and thereby to succeed. The meaning of life in business has everything to do with combining your unique background with real-world opportunities to contribute products and services that others want and need. By doing your part, you make the world a better place to live. You create jobs and thereby allow others to hold their heads high as contributing members of society. The financial rewards you receive are a byproduct of *your* contribution to the world. Few will acknowledge your true value, but your *success* is essential to the success of the world. Without you, the future is bleak.

Let's step back and consider what success really is. It's not necessarily the accumulation of wealth. Economic prosperity may come as a result of what we do, but when it does, it is most often an indirect result. In the real world, those who make significant contributions to society are not always rewarded with financial success. On the other hand, those who focus exclusively on how much money they can make, often end up wasting their lives jumping from one "get rich quick scheme" to another. Some people believe that if our *only* goal is wealth, we are unlikely to do the right things to achieve it. That philosophy was eloquently unfolded by Viktor Frankl (1905-1997), who successfully survived four Nazi death camps, including Auschwitz and Dachau.

Where am I going? Where you go in this life is largely up to you. If you do the right things and do them well for a long enough time, as surely as the spring follows the winter, you will succeed. Economic success *may* follow also. If I were to give my version of Frankl's philosophy, it might be something like this, "don't spend your time in search of the meaning of life; spend your time filling your life with meaning."

As you go about your task, failure will be an inevitable part of your life, but it should not automatically be a discouragement. Why? Because learning *which* are the right things to do and learning *how* to do them is a process. Second, the person who has never failed has no idea what his potential is because he has never reached far enough to exceed it. If we never fail, it means we have probably not reached our full potential.

The 90-Minute MBA® is intended to help you succeed, to push you to pursue your entrepreneurial passion. If you only remember one thing, let it be that there is a difference between *doing the right things* and *doing things right.*

I hope you have gained some insight into what you have to *do* to create the future you want. You have the tools to create the most insightful Business Plan in the business world. You have strategies to reduce the risk of failure. You know how to create unparalleled satisfaction in customers and employees. Your entrepreneurial fire has been fueled. You have the tools to succeed, but *success will require action* on your part, not just the acquisition of knowledge.

In the end, you have the opportunity to succeed, but no one is going to *make* you succeed or succeed on your behalf. Your success or failure will be a result of what *you* do. Remember ten words: *If it is to be, it is up to me.*

If you were attending an in-person "commencement," you would receive a virtual diploma, a projected image. Displayed on the screen are the words, "*The symbol for a degree is an elevated zero if it is not followed by action.*"

Your final exam is real life. It's waiting for you. Get an A+. Enough talk. You have things to do—important things!